Life

AND WHAT HAPPENS WHEN WE DIE

ROBERT TODD

Life

And What Happens When We Die

ROBERT TODD

Life And What Happens When We Die

Copyright © 2023 by Robert Todd

Paperback ISBN: 978-1-63812-848-9
Ebook ISBN: 978-1-63812-849-6

All rights reserved. No part in this book may be produced and transmitted in any form or by any means, electronic, or mechanical, including photocopying, recording, or by any information storage and retrieval system, without permission in writing from the copyright owner.

The views expressed in this work are solely those of the author and do not necessarily reflect the views of the publisher. It hereby disclaims any responsibility for them.

Published by Pen Culture Solutions   10/31/2023

Pen Culture Solutions
1-888-727-7204 (USA)
1-800-950-458 (Australia)
support@penculturesolutions.com

The opinions expressed in this book are my interpretation of the facts gathered over many years as a trainer and clinical hypnotherapist practising in the area of past life regression solving phobias and other problems. I hope it helps you to understand in a simplistic way what this Earth and the Spirit World is all about.

ACKNOWLEDGEMENTS

I would like to thank everyone who assisted me in the preparation of this book particularly my wife Judy, who supported and helped me become the person I am today..

Contents

                                                  Page

1. **Introduction** 8
2. The Reunion 12
3. Why Do We Like Certain Artwork 16
4. Rivers Of Reaction 21
5. Victim Status Or Positive Mind 27
6. Some Situations Are Perceived Differently 33
7. Logical Decisions In An Emotional World 35
8. Decisions Logical 37
9. Handling Thoughts 43
10. Visualisation And Imagery 51
11. Persuasion 57
12. Solving Personal Problems 61
13. Dealing With The Wrong Problem 65
14. Getting To The Real Problem 71
15. Removing Past Life Problems 75
16. We Ask For Karmic Lessons 79
17. Rejected Not Worthy 81
18. Separation And Rejection 91
19. How One Life Can Affect Current Lives 103
20. Families Can Reincarnate As A Group 105

21	Shut Down To Love	113
22	Would Not Cross Over	117
23	Personality	121
24	Conversation About Understanding God	123
25	The Subject Racism	129
26	How Karma Affects Our Lives	131
27	Lost Herself	137
28	Fight To The Death	143
29	Adoption	147
30	What Happens When We Die?	153
31	**Appendix**	**162**
32	**Main Symbols**	**163**
33	**Solving Problems Using Scenes**	**173**
34	**About the Author**	175

INTRODUCTION

This book will look at the world through the eyes of someone who has realised this world is nothing like we perceive, the world is a big school where we sign in to experience and understand certain emotions and experience different situations.

I guess this is part of what set me on quite a quest to know what life is all about and living in a world of accidents, where things just seem to happen beyond our control, or do we have more control than we perceive.

Often when events take place people can have a totally different perspective and make decisions based on their emotions. Do we have control over our life, or is it just the luck of the draw.

I have experienced the world from two aspects, one very logical and one very emotional. I was raised in a world where religion played a part in my early life, then I moved away and became a Spiritualist.

Then I came upon a statement which made me reconsider the whole concept of life.

WHATEVER YOU CAN CONCEIVE AND BELIEVE YOU CAN ACHIEVE

I was curious about this and started to investigate mind control, motivation, meditation and other subjects in that area and it opened up a new way of thinking.

I would like to take you on an adventure to explain what I have learned about life and this world.

Maybe you can understand more about the world as perceived through the eyes of an observer of life and past life therapist.

Before I start, I think it's important to mention these days some people tell us past lives do not exist. I know they exist because, with 20 year's experience I have had so many cases, with so many different stories. Also, because during case studies I am directed by my guide to ask strange questions, as my guide tells me what to do and what questions to ask. So many times, when someone tells me something about their life, I will say, I think that's all we need to know. I move on with the advice of my guide. They are with me all the time, I do not insert or make suggestions that point to the outcome. Believe me, the difference in stories no one could make up on the spot, and they describe situations which inevitably lead to the solutions of the problems they have.

Robert

This is a story as told by Thomas.

In this case Thomas is looking for additional life concepts.

Peter is a person who studied the mind and has improved many people's lives.

Thomas and Peter represent me and many of the thousands of wonderful men and women with whom I have worked.

Sometimes people act like Thomas, sometimes like Peter.

This book is about answering questions you may have when it comes to life, so you can be successful and happy.

THE REUNION

I was excited, I was going to reconnect with Peter. I remember the times we spent together talking about Robert's book, *The Secret Language*, which made a great difference to my life. Then there were the times we talked about Robert's book, *Life What It's All About*.

I learnt so much and now I was going to have the opportunity to meet again.

I asked him could we talk about the things he learnt when he was conducting past life therapy, and to my excitement he agreed. So with many questions in mind, I said could we have the first meeting in his office. Peter agreed that would be fine.

I wanted to know if life is planned out, meaning it becomes a matter of fate or accident as some people believe, or are we in control of what happens.

I was also interested in how he became involved in past life regression, hypnotherapy and counselling and was there a particular event or time that changed his life?

I arrived at his office on time and noticed he had new artwork on the wall. I wondered if it was significant to him.

He said yes, every time we select artwork or we have a particular place we enjoy, it is because everything is connected. The style of clothes we wear, the things we collect or have around us are significant and tell people a lot about who we are.

Peter, can you explain why we like certain artwork?

I sure can. Many years ago, I was asked by my guide to create in my mind a special place I could go to when meditating. A place where I felt completely comfortable. Years later I was taught how to interpret the details in my scene. The same principles apply when we select artwork we enjoy, it tends to represent our attitudes at that time.

Let me explain, before a session I would normally get clients to imagine a place they would like to be where they feel calm and relaxed. Then I would carry out a scene analysis, because it gives me a good indication as to where they are in life. Also, a better way to approach their problem. If they are logical, I use more logic, if they are intuitive, I use more intuitive concepts. By doing this I direct my counselling in a way most suitable to them.

I explained this technique fully in the book *Life Start to Finish* and I have included an extract from the book, and the symbols in the back of this book.

Then I will explain the art in my office.

Robert Todd

EXTRACT FROM THE BOOK *LIFE START TO FINISH*

A field with a river and mountains.
Ahead of him a mountain with a snow-capped top.
To his left a river flowing towards the mountains.
A wooden bridge crossing to the left.
Green grass behind him and more grass to the right. He is sitting.
The sun is on the left-hand corner ahead of him.
The lower part of his body is in blue, the top green.

Analysis of Scene

The mountains, of which there are two, indicate he has two goals. The first one is snow-capped, indicating he is looking for knowledge first. The second is further in the future.

River flowing towards the mountains indicates that others he knows are also moving the same way.

As he is sitting, a long-term problem (the wooden bridge) is preventing him getting to his goal of knowledge.

He has blue on the lower part of his body, indicating he has come from a position of love. On the top is green, showing that he wants to find peace.

The sun on the top left-hand side indicates that he is more spiritual.

He could get up and walk on this side of the river, but that would only give him peace. It would not solve the long-term problem or get him to his main objective, knowledge, which is represented by the snow-capped mountain.

Robert Todd

WHY DO WE LIKE CERTAIN ARTWORK

Thomas, if we look at the features starting from the front of the image, there is a river with a boat. On the right side, some very tall trees and behind a small landmass and shore. On the left-hand side are trees with buildings in front and in the background in the distance, you can see a snow-covered mountain.

This appeals to me because there is water directly in front which shows involvement with people. The right-hand side of the image represents logic, and there are people in a boat, which indicates that I accept people when they provide logical concepts.

The tall trees on the right indicate that I am happy making logical decisions.

The left-hand side of the artwork represents the intuitive area of my mind. On the left the trees are slightly smaller and further into the artwork indicating I am at ease and have developed my ideas over a longer period of time.

The shoreline having houses or buildings indicates I enjoy different options presented to me.

Directly ahead I see an area of trees which are peaceful and will present new knowledge coming to me.

Then the snow-covered mountain is in full view, this is my goal and represents knowledge I am striving to obtain.

So let's look at another image, a beach scene.

Firstly, fairly smooth water. This indicates they do not like arguments. If the beach had large waves, it would indicate they have no problem handling the situation that gets intense (arguments).

With very tiny waves at the edge, this shows they have some beliefs, and are quite willing to put them forward calmly.

On the right of the person there are trees with no way through, indicating a barrier to logic. A rock also on their right indicates there is a short-term problem they need to handle.

If they see this person as themself, sitting on their own, this indicates they prefer to relax by themself and do not need the distraction of others.

Next we have a third painting or artwork that I will analyse.

In this painting there is a large log across the way, and wood means a long-term problem they need to solve. On the right-hand side, they have snow and that indicates they have all the knowledge they need.

The trees behind on the right-hand side indicate they are at ease with their logic. The same on the left-hand side, shows that although it indicates a barrier, they are at ease with their intuition and have a pathway through. This indicates they can move forward easily once they overcome or ignore the long-term problem, the log.

Next if you look between those two sets of trees, there is more snow and behind, trees, indicating they will use logic to solve their problems.

RIVERS OF REACTION

Quite often we have situations in our life where we seem to have little control, such things as likes and dislikes, money, possessions, relationships, and other situations.

We seem to be emotionally locked into a position where we have no control. If we come from a poor family or a rich family, we seem to have totally different attitudes to money.

This is probably one of the easiest ones to explain. We often accept the expectations and attitudes of our culture and family. If you do not make a decision to change this you will end up with the same results. Sometimes people say children got into the wrong company and this is what is causing the problem. Well, all this comes down to attitude, the way we think.

Attitude controls the autonomic nervous system within our mind. We can live in a positive world with many solutions and be able to handle all types of situations or we could also be born into a situation where we are almost doomed to fail. Yet at any time we can change this when we are aware of how the mind works. So, I'm going to talk about what I refer to as the *Rivers of Reaction*. Let's take a typical situation that can happen to anyone and show you how the mind processes that information. Let's assume you are walking or driving into a car park and you see a black cat. How does the mind process this? First we have the outside event which then transfers to the *Rivers of Reaction* within the brain and you draw a conclusion either positive or negative according to your previous experience, family attitude or culture. Imagine you don't like black cats.

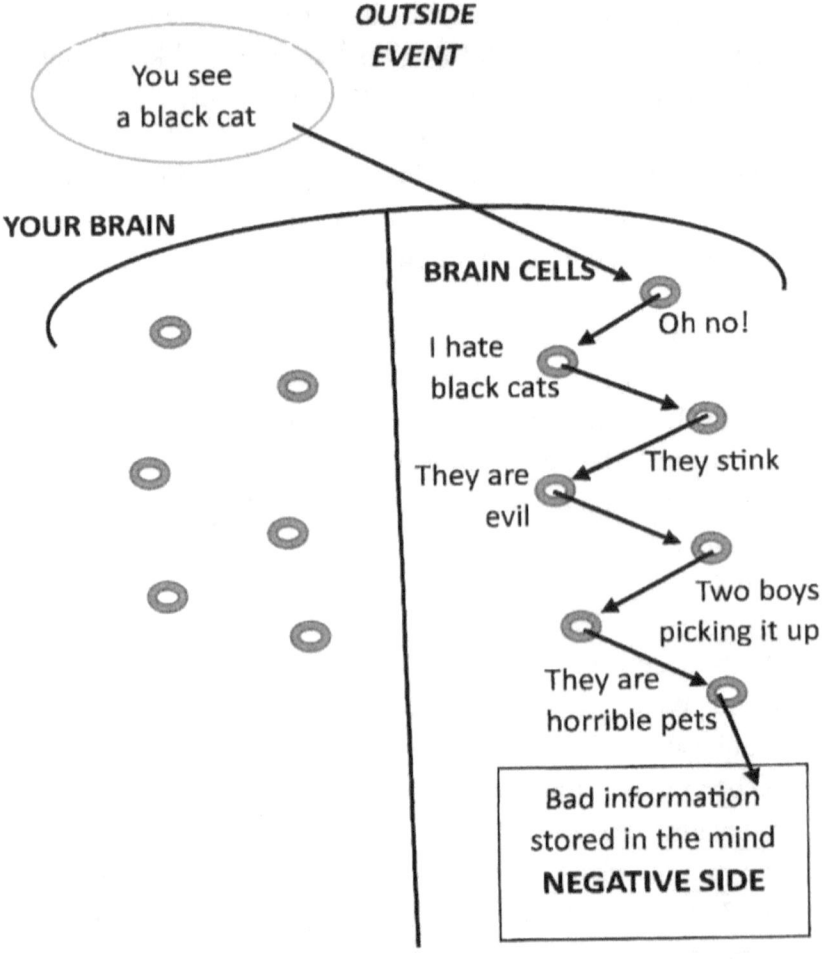

In this case it has been a totally automatic process to the negative. From now on it will follow that pattern every time you see a black cat.

You also have *Rivers of Reaction* to many other things such as the friends you choose, the car you drive, the clothes you wear, money, even success or failure. Once you have formed an attitude as to who you are and how you act in specific situations.

Of course, you can change this any time, by being aware of that initial trigger point which starts the *River of Reaction*. In fact, you have probably done this many times in your life.

Marketing and advertising tends to tell you what you should think. Often your friends tell or show you how to act, also the universe presents you with situations that bring up positives and negatives.

If you find a negative situation or negative feelings come into your life, you should ask yourself what is the fear. This will enable you to run down the *Rivers of Reaction* finding out what fear is in your mind and this enables you to reprogram your mind so that you act positively instead of negatively.

Now let's look at the alternative situation, you have been brought up to like white Persian cats.

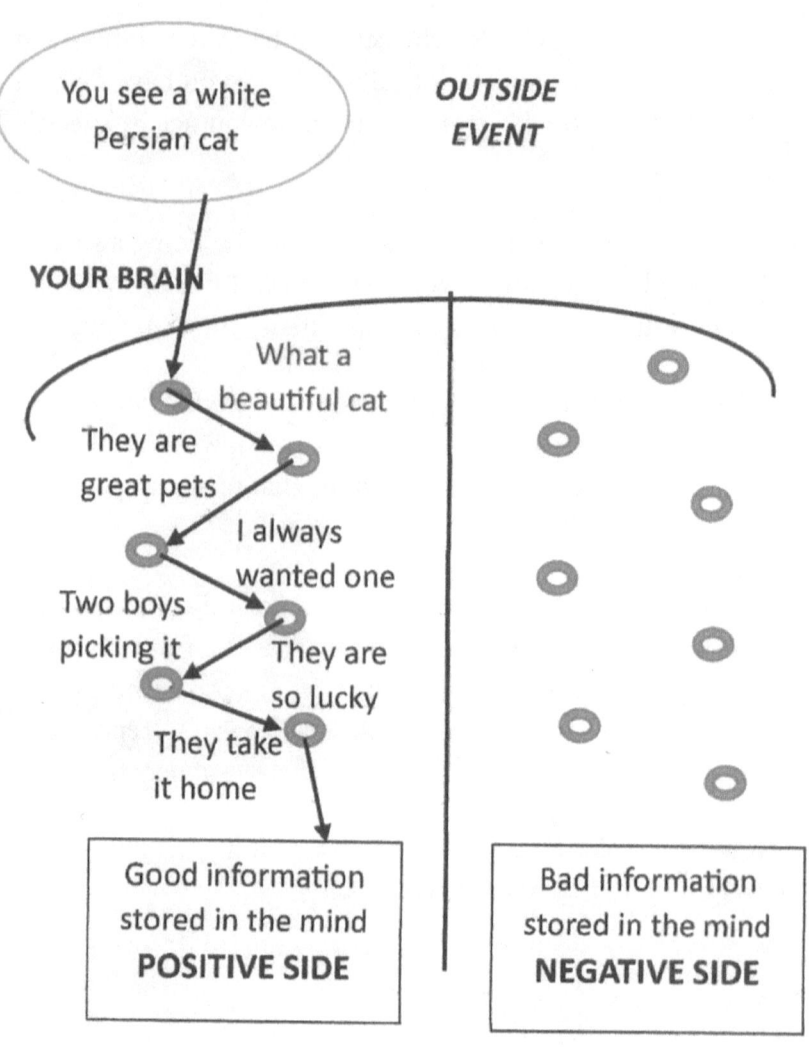

Again it is totally automatic. This time down the positive side of the mind giving you a positive result.

Fortunately, this is also what takes place when it comes to making decisions about anything. If you are in the positive mind, you will always have positive solutions, if you are in the negative mind, you will always have negative solutions.

How do you change this once you become aware. If you have a money problem and you always react negatively and feel it is something out of your reach, obviously you are continually going down the negative side of the mind.

If you want to be a champion swimmer, you would not take advice from people who are still doing dog paddle. If you want to buy a house, you would not discuss with people who continually complain about how they will never own a home of their own.

A suggestion, you change the people you have around you, find people who are successful with money, as you talk to them, you understand the way they think, you can reprogram your mind, your *Rivers of Reaction* to act positively.

So, if you are deciding to buy a new home or want to understand how to, maybe you should be talking to people who know how to do it and own their home or even a few.

If you start simple, gradually you will find you will become competent and your mind will always be running down the *Rivers of Reaction* that give you positive solutions and attitudes that help you with your finances.

The same applies to any other activity, because by doing this you will be changing your attitude and increasing the number of options in the positive mind, filling it with many alternatives and ways to achieve success.

ROBERT TODD

> YOU WILL BE HAPPIER
> IF YOU
> LIVE IN THE POSITIVE SIDE
> OF THE MIND

VICTIM STATUS OR POSITIVE MIND

Victim status

Very few people are aware of what they concentrate on is what they get, so when it comes to the Rivers of Reaction if you concentrate on a negative world, you will find the universe always, without judgement, gives you what you ask for.

What some people continually think about and complain about, for instance, how unfair the world is, how your friends are never reliable, how your family or friends treat you wrong and let you down all the time, how society does not understand or support you, how you are always short of money, how it is impossible to own your own home or find cheap rent. If you continue to live with the feeling that you are a victim, you will be.

Everything that could go wrong will in many situations. If you anticipate problems in your life, more likely than not, they will occur. For example, one day or night when you are out and you drink a little more than you intended, as you drive your car home, you may even think, will I get home safely, and strangely enough that will be the day they had a police car or breath test unit on the way home. You hoped you could get away with it, but knowing your luck, you would probably be caught.

Robert Todd

This is how the universe works, what you think, what you say and what you fear, you get. What a friend tells you could go wrong, will probably happen, and you think the world hates you, then it will. You are a victim and you are out to prove it, continually complaining about your life, and you wonder why it goes wrong.

Well the universe is giving you what you ask for. If you say you are a victim, the universe has many ways to satisfy your request, with unconditional love and without judgement or favour.

Let me give you a very simple example of how the rivers of reaction work negatively even if you change your situation. In a factory there was a young man working and he was very very successful in his job, probably the best operator they had, but all the time while he was in that job, he complained about management. According to him, all managers are aggressive, rude and did not fully understand the job.

It came to pass that his manager got promoted, therefore the management position in his section became vacant. He was considered by management and his workers the most suitable person for the job, because of the quality of his work, he was promoted into the management position.

Within months, the complaints started coming in. Now as manager, he was becoming aggressive, impatient and blaming the workers for incompetence to the point where management above him decided they had made the wrong choice and were going to demote him back to his original job and promote one of the other workers.

Unfortunately for him the other workers did not want him back as they had all grown to dislike him and his attitude. Of course what had happened was, when he was promoted to manager, his River of Reaction or subconscious mind shifted to the program of a manager, which meant he had to be what he believed managers were, aggressive and rude. Because of this and his negative belief system, he lost his job in the company.

Positive mind

On the other hand, if you are positive about life and decide that you can achieve whatever you want if you believe, whatever the mind can conceive and believe, can be achieved. (and here is the key point, *you must believe*).

So how do we do this. First, we must learn to visualise and organise our mind in such a way that as we come up with ideas, we must build a River of Reaction that leads us to a positive confident solution. That does not mean you have to know how it will happen; you must trust the universe to know, it will bring the things into your life that you need to achieve success.

Let me help you with some very simple techniques that have been used by many successful people.

The first one is what is referred to as a vision board. You find yourself a place in your house where you can set up a whiteboard or a pin board where you can write or place photographs, pictures or drawings, the physical things you would like to come into your life, such as a car, a home, particular job, even the income you would like. Now remember the key, it must be something you believe and something you really want and can utilise.

You cannot put up a pipe dream you think would be nice, but you do not believe is possible. It's like you are just putting up a wish list of things that would be nice. The universe does not respond to this. It is no good thinking you will test the technique because the universe knows what's going on. It cannot be tested and if you trust, it will work.

Another technique called visualisation. This one sounds very simple, you are sending a message to the universe of what you want. It is important that you do not treat it as something you need, because the universe thinks if you need something there is a fear, and it will stop the end result taking place so that you learn the lesson there is nothing to fear. On the other hand, if it is what you really want and you believe you are worthy of having, the universe is always willing to give you the things you ask for. So, visualise the situation or event that you would like to take place.

The key to this one is you must visualise it as if it already is, not what you think would take place to make it happen, but the end result. Do not visualise how you are going to get there as the universe has many ways you have never thought of to achieve the end result. It may even realise you need other information, techniques or abilities to be able to reach your end result. It will take you on a journey to get new skills, understandings and beliefs that will enable you to achieve the result you're looking for.

Once you have the visualisation end result in your mind, you must reinforce it by adding the emotions you will feel when it is actually achieved, and finally you must repeat this exercise regularly. The more you exercise your mind and belief in the universe this way, the universe will act much quicker. When you are first using these techniques, the universe needs to reprogram you to the belief and confidence that you need to achieve the results you want. Be patient, if you have asked for something, the universe is working on it.

You cannot do this as a whim, you must use your desire to have total understanding of the power of the universe.

Start simple, but that does not mean you do not have your long-term goals. One of the first techniques I learnt was to program for parking spots, then taught many people how to do this by visualising where you want to park, then go there and park.

Either way if you think I'll just try this, it won't work. You must have the belief and faith that it will happen, you cannot test the universe or use it for the purposes of ego.

I will summarise. Visualise what you want as if it has already happened, feel the emotion involved when it's achieved and do it regularly, reinforce the image until it becomes reality.

AS YOU TALK AND AS YOU THINK THIS BECOMES YOUR LIFE'S REALITY

SOME SITUATIONS ARE PERCEIVED DIFFERENTLY

Thomas, often when events take place, people can have a totally different perspective and make decisions based on their emotions which can affect their entire lives.

Peter, can you give us an example of that?

I can. A father who was religious died at a young age. He had two sons. They could believe God took their father to punish them, or they can decide their father died because he failed to have a check-up with a doctor, instead of just eating Rolaids which are for heartburn.

Well one blamed God for taking his father. The other decided that his father should have taken greater responsibility for his health. These decisions affected their entire lives.

I am not saying which is right or wrong, in fact they are probably both right for their life's objectives and lessons. This can happen if they are Buddhist, Islamic, Jewish, Christian, Atheist or any other belief, yet that decision changes their prospective of life and death.

GOD

OFTEN GETS BLAMED FOR MANY THINGS WHEN IT'S OUR CHOICE

LOGICAL DECISIONS IN AN EMOTIONAL WORLD

Peter, we seem to make decisions more emotionally than logically.

You're right, most of us have a belief system which is established over many years, many lifetimes, when we are in the womb, when we are first born. There are many traditions we are born into, because of different cultures and their influence. Then we tend to learn through experience and logical reasoning.

Peter, are you saying this world is emotional yet we try to make logical decisions?

Thomas, we can make a logical decision about building or buying a house, how many bedrooms, how many bathrooms, yet when it comes to design, colours and furniture, emotions become involved. Logic may work with physical things and ideas, but it is very difficult when we add the emotions of love or fear, which is what this planet is based on. Yet, we tell people to use logic even when making emotional decisions.

Thomas, I am talking about logic at a conference next week, maybe you would like to come.

ROBERT TODD

**THIS WORLD IS BASED ON
LOVE AND FEAR
THESE AFFECT
BOTH
LOGIC AND EMOTIONS**

DECISIONS LOGICAL

The next week I attended Peter's conference and photographed some of the diagrams he used.

Now I would like to present a summary of what Peter said.

Let's look at logic and how it works. We can look at the mind as a set of scales on which we place facts on one side and the opposing facts on the other side.

We already have facts on the scales from a previous life. In many cases this is what we came to change. Then we add family influences, and friends.

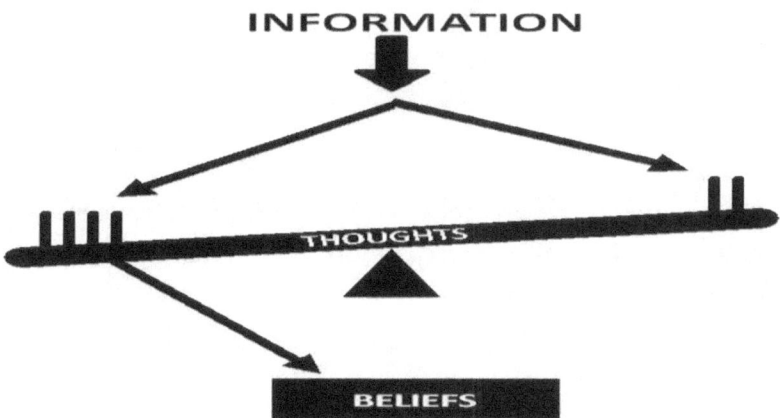

As we keep getting facts and there are more facts on the other end of the scales, then obviously we would have to change beliefs?

To prevent that we build an attitude above the scales biased towards the weakest side.

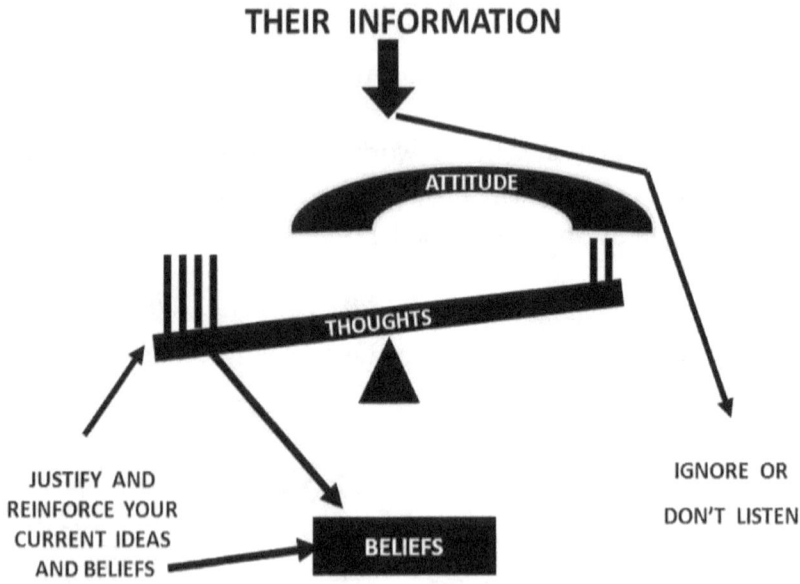

Unfortunately, we are not open to new ideas or concepts, so now we are becoming more emotional, and making decisions based on our attitude.

On earth we need to be an open-minded sceptic and move our attitude to a central position so information can get on both sides of the scales.

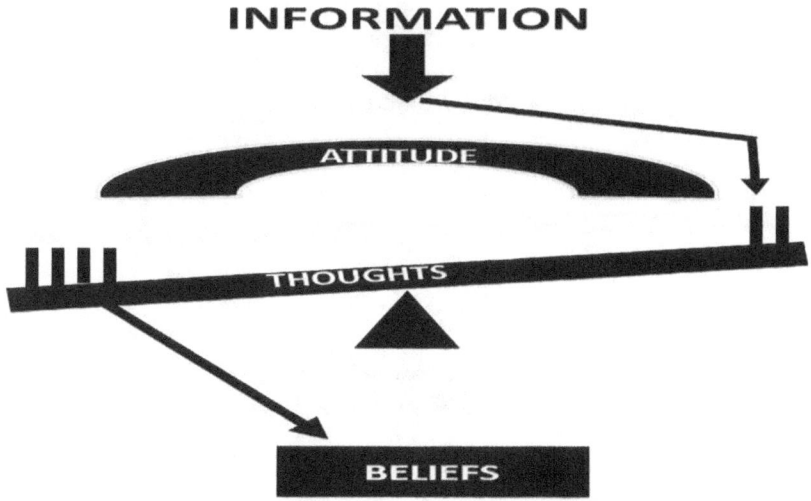

When we do this, we can gather new information that may help us to overcome our fears, and receive alternatives and advice that we can put on the scales.

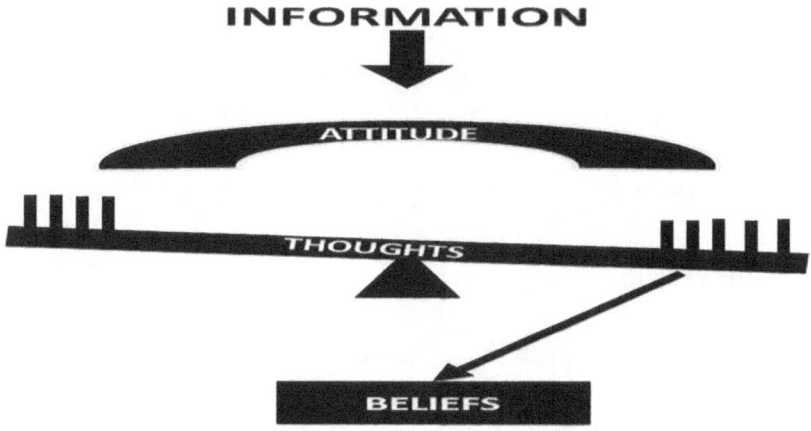

Once we have achieved this, our attitude will unfortunately move again to protect our new beliefs.

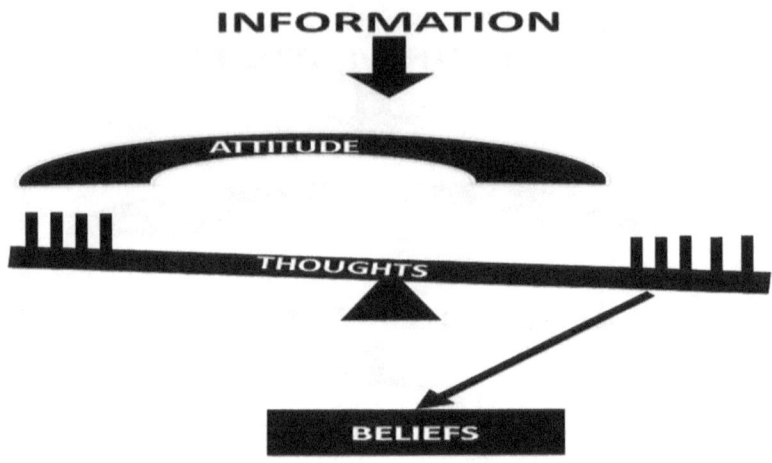

You are only aware of 10 per cent. The rest are part of your unknown belief system, and it works automatically.

Logic is okay for some things, but when emotions are involved, we can't understand why we don't feel comfortable with the logical decision.

We often think we work something out logically. Yet quite often if we do not have all the information necessary, we can make assumptions that are not necessarily true.

Then Peter told a joke, one I have heard him tell before. I think it explains exactly what he means, so I think it is worth telling again.

A gambler was deciding on which horse to place a bet in the next race. He decided to stand near the starting gates and see which horse went into the barrier easily, hoping that this would indicate to him a winning horse. As the horses were put in, a priest raced across to the horses, took a small book from his pocket, placed his hand on one of the horses, then he left and jumped back over the fence and waited. The starting gates opened. The horses bolted out. The race seemed to go quite quickly, and the horse the priest put his hand on won.

The gambler thought, this is great. I must see what's going on here. Maybe it is something I need to know.

In the next race once again, the priest raced across to a horse, took out his book, placed his hand on the horse, read from the book, placed it back in his pocket, and jumped over the fence. The race started, and lo and behold, there was a bit of a struggle, but the priest's horse won.

Well, the guy thought this is amazing, so he watched very carefully. Once again, the priest jumped over the fence, raced along, put his hand on one of the horses.

Then the guy raced up and put everything he had on the horse to win. He got back just in time to see the horses bolt out of the starting gates. The horse that the priest put his hand on seemed to be doing well, then all of a sudden it stumbled and fell over and died.

The guy could not believe this, so he went up to the priest and said, 'What is going on? The first time you put your hand on the horse, it won. The second time you put your hand on the horse, it won. The third time, the horse drops dead?'

The priest looked at him and said, 'My son, my son, are you a Catholic?'

Robert Todd

The gambler said, 'What difference does that make?'

And the priest said, 'You can't tell the difference between a blessing and the last rites.'

Quite often when we think we are using logic and do not have all the facts, we can draw conclusions that are not necessarily correct.

After the session I asked Peter if there were any other subjects he lectured on. Peter said yes, things such as handling thoughts, visualisation and imagery and persuasion and to my excitement he gave me a copy of his notes, which I have included.

After the meeting Peter asked if we could meet in about a weeks' time. We arranged to meet at a park opposite his office where they have outside seating.

**IN THIS WORLD
YOU SHOULD BE
AN
OPEN MINDED SCEPTIC**

HANDLING THOUGHTS

Your thoughts, positive and negative control your life. *If **you** want to control your life, you must control your thoughts.* You must be able to eliminate the negative thoughts and concentrate on positive thoughts, only then do we get positive results. If you allow negative thoughts, you're going to get negative results. It's that simple.

Negatives come from different sources: -
Culturally Imposed, People Imposed and Personally Imposed

Let's start with the CULTURALLY IMPOSED

All through history people have developed statements to suit the situations and circumstances they encounter, then they tell us these statements are fact. Others then base their lives on these so-called beliefs and we think they are true and act them out, and they become true.

Such things as 'life wasn't meant to be easy'. It's an expression of their personal belief system. It may be true for them, but it doesn't have to be true for you. Here are some examples you may have heard, or even use -
    Money doesn't grow on trees
    Money is the root of all evil
    Nothing comes without hard work
    You must have the bad, to appreciate the good
    Win some, lose some

Too good to be true
Good times can't last forever
and I guess the classic for a lot of people,
Wear clean underwear in case you get hit by a bus

These are called truisms.

Another area of Culturally Imposed, is proverbs. How many times have you heard, fools rush in where angels fear to tread or, look before you leap. These mean hold off and be careful.

Then there is, a stitch in time saves nine or, he who hesitates is lost. Now these tell us we should move now.

So we've got proverbs that say hold back and we've got proverbs that say move now. You know they can't both be true. The difficulty arises when people base their life on certain proverbs. If one person believes, he who hesitates is lost and their partner believes, fools rush in where angels fear to tread, one is wanting to move and the other wanting to hesitate, this is where many conflicts arise.

What we are doing is basing our lives on these concepts - when we act them out, they become real. Statements like 'life wasn't meant to be easy', and proverbs have become truisms, so what do we do?

Well, the answer is, STOP. Sit down and say to yourself, do I want this to be true for me? If you want to accept it, that's fine. If not, throw it away.

Realise it's just a statement someone imposed on you.

Truisms can control your life and while they control your life, *you have no control.* So, get rid of the society-imposed negatives.

PEOPLE IMPOSED NEGATIVES.

This is where people make a statement and then look for agreement.

A typical one is first thing in the morning when it's raining, someone says, oh, it's a lousy day because it's raining, they want you to agree. Of course, if you accept it's a lousy day, then it certainly can turn out that way.

What about when people come up to you with a particular situation and say, oh you're going to have difficulty finding a solution here, they're asking you to agree. If you say, oh yeah, it'll be tough, it could turn out that way, and they were right. You see, these are the People Imposed. They want agreement. All these statements impose negative thoughts on us.

Are you going to allow them to control your life or do you want to be in control? If you want to control your life, you must control people-imposed negatives.

Now we're going to give you two ways to get control.

The first technique is, CUT IT OFF.

That means cut it off, and don't let it go on. So the next time you find someone says to you, you'll find this difficult, or they may say, meetings are a waste of time, as soon as you hear a statement like that, make a bland comment, something like, 'oh, that's interesting or I understand why you say that'. In other words you tend to agree with the person, but in words that do not allow it to be imposed on you. You do not accept it as true, and you do not even consider it.

Don't visualise what the problem could be, just simply say in your own mind, that is that person's view and I am going to make my own decision. So you make the simple statement, 'fine, ok', and then just leave it. Start making your own decision. Remember, CUT IT OFF, and make a bland statement.

The second technique is BEEN THERE, DONE THAT
This is where, if you're in a particular situation where people continue to tell you *the same bad news*. How do you handle it when it's going on continually?

You stop, sit down, and you say to yourself 'what is the absolute worst thing that could happen in this situation?'
Then you say to yourself 'Ok, what would I do then?' Once you have made a decision of what is the worst that could happen and have the answer, from then on every time someone brings up the subject you say, 'I know, thank you, or fine', then in your own mind you say, been there, done that and I know what to do.

Now by doing that, you take the power away from the thought. You're saying, I can handle the situation. The fascinating part is, people often worry over things that never happen. So don't get involved in these types of situations.

The third type of negative, PERSONALLY IMPOSED.

These are the ones we carry around with us all the time. They are situations and circumstances and the words we use every day.

Everything I eat goes to fat, it makes me sick, I'm no good until after morning tea, I can't seem to get started in the morning, I should tidy my desk, I have nothing but bad luck, I have nothing to wear.

Perhaps we have a fear, or a doubt, and we say I don't know if I can handle this, or I don't know what to do.

For example:
We're having a party and we start worrying, will things turn out right? Will everybody turn up? I'm not sure what to do, and the whole thing gets on top of us. Maybe you are trying to cook this special meal and you're not sure it will turn out ok, you wonder if the recipe will work, you hope everything's going to be ok. These are the type of doubts that come into our mind. We have these pre-conditioned tapes, programs that cause us a problem, because we've had them before.

So how do we handle these?

I will give you 4 techniques.
The first one is called BECOME THE OBSERVER

As soon as you realize you are experiencing a negative thought, as soon as you realize you've got caught up in it, you simply step back from the situation and say to yourself, what is happening to me is, I am having a negative thought. You look at yourself and say, oh boy! Am I glad I'm not getting caught up in that. You actually observe yourself involved in the negative. Observe the doubt, pull yourself away. By pulling yourself away, the thought loses its power because you don't get emotionally involved and the negative can't survive.

The next technique is EXAGGERATION.

For example if you were having a special dinner, you're cooking a new recipe, and you're worried whether the recipe will work out. Then you're sitting there saying to yourself, oh, if this recipe fails, I will look like a fool.

Then to exaggerate you say, not only will the recipe fail, but it will blow up in the oven and all the ingredients will run out of the oven onto the kitchen floor. When others see it, they'll say to themselves, look at all this mess over the floor, how could anyone be that bad a cook? Then it'll ooze down the hallway and out into the street, it'll run down the road, they'll have to bring in the fire brigade.

By this time of course, as I said, the mind starts defends itself, it says no fire brigade, it won't even get down the hall, it won't get on the kitchen floor, what happens if it blows up in the oven? It won't blow up in the oven and then of course you realise it may just fail, but then again, it may be a great success.

You can have a lot of fun with the Exaggeration. Also, just another side issue. They say that if something goes wrong, in five years you'll laugh about it. You'll laugh about the party that was ruined by the recipe that failed. Well, why not sit back now and laugh about it if it does fail? It really isn't that much of a disaster.

The next technique
COUNTERACT IT WITH THE EXACT OPPOSITE.

That means as soon as a thought comes into mind, the recipe will fail, you say the recipe will succeed.

You counteract it with the exact opposite statement. The mind can only hold one thought at any one time.

I have some very simple statements I make every time someone says something to me that may be negative. If people say things like, gee, people are finding business is getting bad, I have a statement that says, that's great, in tough times my company succeeds. It is also important to have a statement that always keeps you in good health so when someone says, how are you today, I say, good always. If someone says to you, oh, the flu is going around, I say, that's interesting, and then I say to myself, I'm always healthy. So I have a series of very simple statements that counteract the negative, with the exact opposite.

The next technique AFFIRMATIONS.

Affirmations are statements that you make over and over, and they cram the mind, and the mind eventually wakes up to the fact that they are true.

Emil Coue was a doctor who healed people by using affirmations. He worked on people who in fact could not be healed by anybody else. He used an affirmation that I'm sure you have heard, the affirmation was, every day in every way, I'm getting better and better. Patients were told to say this statement 24 times each time before a meal. He healed many patients using conventional medicine and affirmations. Affirmations are far more powerful than many people believe possible.

If you say, I feel peaceful and calm, and you repeat it over and over, you'll find it becomes reality.

When you get in the shower in the morning have an affirmation, such as, it's going to be a great day. If you're sitting at the traffic lights, you can use affirmations while you are waiting. Don't waste time fill it with affirmations.

How many times should you say something? Well, I would suggest about 20 times a day. So make affirmations for each type of activity that you do.

THE REST IS UP TO YOU

VISUALISATION AND IMAGERY

Visualisation and imagery are one of the most important mind tools you can use today. You can improve your life by achieving the things you want through learning to use your subconscious mind to full advantage.

Imagine you are fishing from a boat out in the ocean. The boat has a steering wheel and an automatic pilot. You set the automatic pilot so the boat heads in a northerly direction, at about two to three knots. You're sitting at the back of the boat, unfortunately not catching any fish, you decide to make a change in your direction. You move to the front of the boat, take hold of the steering wheel and change the direction, steering the boat towards the east. You have overridden the automatic pilot. If you let go the steering wheel and go back to fish, the boat will slowly turn back to the northerly direction. The automatic pilot takes over and returns the boat back to the original compass setting. You could have changed the direction of the boat without even touching the steering wheel by changing the automatic pilot, the boat would then gradually adjust to its new compass heading.

Your self-image, your automatic pilot, is programmed to behave and respond automatically. Every day you automatically do, think, and feel according to the way your automatic pilot, that's the self-image, has been programmed.

One day you decide to make a change in your direction, so you get hold of the behaviour which is like grabbing the steering wheel and head yourself in a new direction.

For example giving up smoking, as long you consciously hold onto the steering wheel you are all right. The moment you forget to exert conscious effort and let go of your behaviour, you return right back to the old habits, the old characteristics of being a smoker.

If you are overweight, maybe your automatic pilot is set at 10 kilos heavier than you want to be. You decide to lose weight, you steer yourself away from the old image by grabbing the steering wheel changing your diet and using other techniques yet the moment you let go, you go back to the old image overweight. This is why so many diets fail.

Now when you're holding the steering wheel there is tremendous tension on the system, you're holding yourself away from your subconscious image. When you force change you try to override the image of yourself, this creates tremendous tension and strain. Consequently many times people create headaches and illness because they are attempting to be different to their self-image.

Once you learn to reset your self-image you no longer need to try to override your self-image. You can use the tools of visualisation and imagery to reset your self-image. You are able to be the person you want to be, to improve your family life and your working life.

The subconscious mind has no contact with the outside world, the information it processes is the information provided by the conscious mind. Therefore, when you visualise something, the subconscious mind cannot tell the difference between that and reality.

At the conscious level you know what is going on. You can tell the difference between the experience of doing something in the physical world and doing it in the mental world but the subconscious mind cannot tell the difference.

Whenever you visualise something, you generate in yourself the emotional response to the visualisation and that passes from the conscious to the subconscious and the subconscious will act on it as if it is true.

For example, one day you are looking in the newspaper you see an advertisement for the circus. It states that they have a special lion exhibit, you decide to go and see the lions. When you arrive, you find at the side of the big tent, a large cage with a tarpaulin over it, obviously this is the cage where the lions are kept.

You lift the cover, the cage is dark, you look into the back of the cage and see an old chewed bone on the floor, the cage is empty. Your eyes peer into the darkness under the cover and you see the door of the cage is open. At that precise moment you feel a heavy weight on your shoulder and the image of a lion comes into your mind. You imagine a lions paw is on your shoulder, at the same time you hear the roar of a lion, and feel the hot breath on your neck. The conscious mind immediately thinks it's a real lion and sends a message to the subconscious, it reacts by increasing your heart rate, your pulse and your blood pressure. You drop the tarpaulin expecting to see a lion, only to find it's a friend playing a joke.

In this case the subconscious mind acted to the message that there was a lion and the physical actions and emotions took place automatically. Your subconscious mind acts on an imaginary experience, the same as a real experience, it cannot tell the difference. It also produces the feelings associated with that image. All images are stored in the subconscious mind and affect your self-image.

Your self-image, your abilities and inadequacies, are an accumulation of all the experiences you have had in your life, these experiences may be actual or imaginary.

If you want to change yourself, if you want an ability you don't have, you use visualisation with emotional content to reprogramme the subconscious mind, the self-image, to what you want.

Not just any image will change your self-image, there is a particular way visualisation and imagery must be used. If any type of imagery would change you, then every time you watch television or a great sportsman, every time you admired someone else achieving something, you would be installing that into your subconscious and therefore altering your self-image. This does not happen because you must use imagery and imagination in a very specific way.

The type of imagery necessary to create change is referred to as experiential imagery. This is where you see yourself in the role.

For example, you can watch a great tennis player and say, isn't he brilliant, or say he can achieve wonders on the tennis court. You may see a successful manager and admire that person and admire their characteristics. At this stage you are only imaging them achieving, you must see yourself carrying out the activity of a great tennis player or as a successful manager. To see someone else doing it is not adequate.

It must be in the first person, you must be seeing in your mind you actually carrying out the activity, with feeling. If you see yourself as a warm loving member of a family, if you visualise yourself and add the emotions, then this will imprint on your subconscious mind.

All meaningful long-term change starts on the inside. It must start at the subconscious level, you must use experiential imagery and then go over and over it until you accept it in the subconscious, then it becomes easy for you to carry out the activity.

The rules are, it must be in the first person, seeing yourself in the present tense, you must feel the emotions involved and repeat it regularly.

In fact, you have used this type of imagery all your life. Every time you carry out an activity and it is confirmed that you were a success or failure, the image automatically transferred to the subconscious, the self-image.

Now you can deliberately control the development of your self-image rather than allowing it to happen. Once you have gained control of your subconscious, you have the power to develop your own characteristics and become the person you want to be.

All the best, Success, Happiness, Wealth, the Rest of Your Life

Robert Todd

**FIRST PERSON
WITH EMOTION
AND REGULARLY**

PERSUASION

If you use persuasion to the detriment of others, then you have created a karma debt for yourself to pay in this life or the next. What you put out you get back. That is Karma.

There are a few techniques I have used on many occasions. If you are giving a speech you can use a formular of past, present and future, or problem, cause and solution. These are fairly simple. On the other hand if you are persuading the formular of FEEL, FELT and FOUND, this technique is more suitable for a discussion with an individual.

FEEL: First this means you need to listen carefully to the person's current beliefs about the situation. Do this by using active listening. Once you fully understand the person's current situation and their solution to the problem, you then feed that information back, to make sure that you fully understand and to reassure them you have listened to what they want to say and do.

Using the statement or an equivalent say, *"so you feel"* and explain to them your full understanding of what they say and feel.

This shows understanding and shows concern for where they are at present.

Then you move to the FELT stage, where you explain you understand and you have had similar feelings in a situation, showing you know where they're coming from. This has to be a real situation.

You never lie. If you listen carefully to what they're talking about, you will have had similar experiences somewhere in your life.

Then you move to the FOUND section of the speech.

You explain how you have changed your opinion, because of something you were told by someone else. This takes away the authority from yourself and may give them a simple reason to change. Then you go on to tell them who and why you have changed. Again, this must be the truth.

Of course your statements must be positive, credible and a plausible solution, understood by them. After this you ask them to *join with you or help you.* If you have explained yourself fully and show an understanding and empathy to their problem, more than likely they will join with you, or help you.

ANOTHER TECHNIQUE

Most suitable if you are in a meeting where you have the option to express an opinion without being interrupted. It is designed to use observation and provide a number of alternatives, almost like you are taking people on an adventure of five different solutions and finally recommend two from which you hope they will select the one you want.

Solution one may be the one they have talked about but you are not overly happy with and can see some faults, although you do not express the faults at this stage.

Solution two is really the one you want. It is expressed in a positive persuasive manner without a lot of the detail.

Solution three is designed to present a solution which actually is slightly better than one, because as you present it, you point out the problems you see with solution one.

Solution four is similar to solution two, where you sell your ideas and is probably not quite as good as solution two.

Solution five is there just to confuse the issue and is usually not even considered as a possible solution. However now people have so much in their mind, they are pretty well confused.

Then you go back to solution two and four and compare them suggesting that solution two is better, because of whatever the advantages you believe and explain in detail.

Hopefully by now the meeting is completely confused and make the decision between the two you are suggesting, because people like to make a decision between only two items once all the others have been discarded, and of course hopefully, they select solution two.

SOLVING PERSONAL PROBLEMS

Peter said our next meeting could be held in the park opposite his office. When I arrived, it was nice and quiet, there were chairs and tables scattered around under large trees. There was a coffee shop nearby so I bought some lunch and coffee then saw Peter coming, he had brought his lunch.

Thomas I want you to remember, if you have a problem in this life, it needs to be solved by you in this life. It is not someone or something that creates the problem. You brought it into this life for a reason.

So Peter, does that apply to all problems big or small?

The problem may or may not be major, the problem is within you and you may need to learn a new attitude, thought or belief.

How do I do that?

Ask yourself, what feeling do I have? What is causing this feeling? Is there a fear, an attitude you have, or it may be an indication this is one of your lessons.

Peter is it necessary, even with small problems?

Well Thomas the universe always starts with a small message and if you don't pay attention they can grow into a major problem. I often say if you break a fingernail, it's an indication something needs to be fixed and if you don't pay attention it may get more drastic. According to Louise Hay each finger represents an emotion or situation in life.

The thumb	Intellect and Worry
Index Finger	Ego and Fear
Middle Finger	Anger and Sexuality
Ring Finger	Unions and Grief
Little Finger	Family

So every time I get upset or cranky it could be a message?

That's correct Thomas, everything that happens in life has a purpose, everything that comes into your life, you bring it to you for self-improvement.

Peter why is it someone I care about, create the things that annoy me most?

Two people can actually look at exactly the same situation and take opposite views. One positive and one negative. The most important thing is what you are learning from every situation. It's not what happens in life, it is how you view it, and how you react. If you change the way you look at things, the things you look at change. Every time you have an emotion, a like or dislike, the dislike is telling you to look at the situation and see what is taking place. Why are you reacting automatically and does it really matter, or is it something that makes us different. Some people like timber furniture, others like glass, gold or chrome. Any preferences could have come from your parents, attitudes in this life, or from experience in a past life.

Thomas mild differences are projected by our personality. Not all phobias create a problem, they are just there because of your past experiences. Of course, phobias can become dramatic and create fear. Each time you find you have negative emotions, it's a good idea to stop, sit down and ask yourself, what is it I fear in this situation?

Peter, sometimes people seem to get cranky for no apparent reason and become aggressive. It seems they have no control. Is this created by a fear?

Many fears can be hidden and could be part of their life's learning. Often we don't realise the universe is putting us in a position where we can get the answers. In fact we are being put in situations and told the answers all the time, this is so we learn.

Peter are our likes and dislikes what make us different and therefore enable us to make choices about who we like and who we don't like?

Thomas, some people find there are certain people they like and certain people they don't like. This, of course could be an emotional opinion (love or fear) or just an attitude we hold, or maybe something we have learned from the family. Quite often we don't know why we like or don't like the person. It can be as simple as the colour of their clothes, the shape of their body, their height, there are many triggers that can come from the past and present lives that create these instant likes or dislikes.

Peter, can you give us a simple example of this?

I remember one time I was asked to find out why a personnel manager had selected a female employee for a particular job in the company, when there was a second female applicant who was far more qualified. Looking at his records and the staff, I realised that he had actually always selected women who had big hips, without him knowing. I was talking to him about life and he mentioned his mother said when you pick a wife pick one with big hips, because they were good for childbirth.

So the opinion he held was in fact influencing him subconsciously and he had always selected women with large hips. Of course, he was unaware of this.

The reason people pick their friends is because of certain characteristics. We do everything for a reason.

If you notice yourself becoming frustrated, depressed or angry, your emotions are telling you this is one of your lessons. If the problem is reoccurring and you are not coming up with a solution that is effective, getting angry, resentful or losing your cool, does not solve the problem. You must look at the fear. Others are mirrors to you. They are there to help you solve your problem, that's why they're in your life.

EVERYTHING IN LIFE HAS A PURPOSE

DEALING WITH THE WRONG PROBLEM

Peter, do people always start out talking about their main problem?

Thomas, this case is a perfect example of dealing with the wrong problem. In a case where a woman could not complete any tasks, she would get close to the end and all of a sudden be depressed upset or cranky and not finish what she had started.

Let's look at extracts from the session so you can see the way it progressed.

I asked her to describe her scene. She said she was in a house and standing on a timber deck, indicating a long-term problem.

W is Client   C. is Counsellor

C.   You are going to see a light surround you and in that light, see a person. This person is your guide, you are completely safe. What is the person's name, listen and tell me what they say?

W.   Jesus

C.   I want you to go back to the original scene standing on the deck. Are you there yet?

W. Yes

C. I want you to place your hands on the deck and go back in time and space, you'll be in a new place, it will be the cause of your problem. I want you to tell me what's going on around you?

W. Back in my home I'm standing on the deck looking out, I'm five years old, l don't know what's expected of me. My brother is riding his skateboard but I can't do that, I keep falling off.

C. How does that make you feel?

W. I'm no good at anything, then I found ballet. I really liked it. When I was 11, I was top of my class and we did a concert and they took a video. I was watching the video later and I realised I was overweight. So I said I hated ballet and I didn't want to do it anymore.

C. Was that true?

W. No, I really loved it, but I didn't like anybody looking at my body.

C. How did that make you feel?

W. Horrible, I really wanted to but I said I didn't and I got very depressed.

C. Is that all we need to know about that scene?

W. Yes

C. Jesus will take us to another time and another place. Now we are going to go back in time and space and where we are going to find out why you had those experiences in this life and why you need to experience depression at that time in life. Where are you now?

W. I am in the country I see a tower, it's a windmill, it's like a desert area.

C. Do you see anyone there?

W. I see a man with a gun, his name is Rowan he's 29 years old.

C. I am going to count to 3 and you will know everything Rowan is feeling as he's walking along the road. What is he feeling?

W. Anger and revenge

C. Why is he feeling anger and revenge?

W. His wife and his little girl were killed in a fire. It was his house got set on fire and he is angry at what happened and is angry at himself because of what happened.

C. Move on and tell us what happened to him?

W. He's walking along the road with a gun.

C. Why does he have a gun?

W. He shot himself.

C.   Can you understand how he got so angry and cranky that he shot himself?

W.   He couldn't see any future, he couldn't move forward that's why he shot himself, there was so much emotion and he gave in to it.

C.   Was that the right decision at the time or was it the wrong decision, what do you think?

W.   He could have gone through it and come out the other side but it would have been very hard.

C.   Do you see how he made the decision on the spot when he was depressed and said he couldn't see any future and said to himself, I can't cope with this anymore I'm out of here?

W.   His mind was going way too fast, and he lost control of his thoughts, he was blaming himself and couldn't see any way out.

C.   Can you forgive him for that, do you understand that? Can you see why he did that and can you forgive him. Ask Jesus to help you. Can you see him lying there, put your hand on his head and say I forgive you.

W.   Yes, I forgive him, for what he did and I understand.

C.   Now go back onto the deck and I want to ask you was the feeling he had the same as the feeling you had when you gave up your ballet. You lied knowing you really wanted to keep going but you couldn't see any other way out.

W. Yes

C. And can you forgive yourself for those feelings? Can you see you needed to understand that you can carry on after those types of feelings?

W. Yes

When she came to me, she stated at about the age of five she saw her brother riding his skateboard, she tried and kept falling off, she made the decision she was inadequate at doing everything.

If we had worked on that we could have missed the real problem, for in the session she brought up the situation in the ballet of her overweight perception. In reality she did not have a major problem with weight. The real issue was the depression she was feeling when things did not go as she wanted. In a previous life, she felt so depressed with events that she committed suicide.

Suicide is not part of a person's program before coming here. Under universal law she needs to come back and experience a similar emotional situation so she can learn to handle her emotions. The universe brings up a problem early in a person's life where they experience a similar emotion and then they go through the depression and come out the other side knowing there are alternatives they need to explore.

She needs to come back and have an experience early in this life with the same feelings of depression and not knowing which way to go. She created the depression by lying about the fact that she hated ballet when in fact it was her passion.

Peter, how did it all finish up?

Now understanding her depression, she knows there are other alternatives and she can work at finishing what she starts.

We went on and discussed the slight overweight problem she had and she decided to use the ballet as exercise and diet to help lose the weight.

> **TELLING LIES WILL NEVER FIX A PROBLEM IT JUST COVERS IT UP**

GETTING TO THE REAL PROBLEM

When someone comes to me and say they have a problem, in many cases they are talking about a symptom and not the real problem.

What do you mean Peter, if they say they're scared of flying, isn't that the real situation?

It may be they are like me. I used to say I had a fear of flying, in fact, I was covering the real problem. The problem was I suffered travel sickness. Nobody but my family knew. Then strangely when I learned to drive a car and got my license, I no longer had the problem, even as a passenger. When I was old enough, I learned to fly. After training I eventually was allowed to take the plane up on my own and strangely enough the fear of being sick went, and also my stated fear of flying.

If you discuss their problem as stated and ignore the real cause, you can actually influence their situation the wrong way. I found that instead of discussing their stated problem I would simply say, "Don't tell me anything, I don't want to be influenced the wrong way". Then when I had analysed their scene, I would put them under a light hypnosis and then say the words "Go back to the cause of your problem".

Peter, do you mean you go back to the real problem not their stated problem?

Yes, I know how I reacted, covering up the real problem. I found it is better if I go beyond what they are telling me, because the true answer to the real problem is already in the person's mind.

Peter, is that what you talked about before, a phobia in this life and they have no idea where it comes from?

Well done, Thomas the problem can be in this life however in many cases the problem was in a past life.

Peter, can you give an example of someone with the fear of flying?

Yes, a woman came to me with the fear of flying. This was a symptom. I ignored that situation and using a very light form of hypnosis, I went directly to the mind to find out what was the real fear. The real cause turned out to be that she had difficulty making a decision and telling herself to take the trip.

It was not the fear of flying. The fear was, making the wrong decision. Would she make the right decision. She had made previous decisions which turned out to be wrong.

Peter, that was great, do you have another example?

Thomas, I think I told you about this one in a previous book, so let's remind you. A woman who came to see me and said she wanted to leave her husband. He was driving her crazy by persistently asking questions. Every time she decided to leave, she was not able to do so. I was not suggesting and never would suggest she should or should not leave, because that would mean helping her make the move that may be wrong.

The problem was she had a previous life where she was on her own and a very lonely old woman when she died. This was holding her back from leaving. The real problem was she had the same partner in a previous life and the relationship in that life was affecting her situation in this life. So the problem was not her having the strength to leave, she was required to solve the problem in her relationship.

Often when people have a problem in a relationship the first solution they come up with is to leave. This means they are not actually solving their problem and they just move to the next relationship with the same problem.

Unless they solve the real problem, they will not be able to enjoy life. Solve the problem before you leave and you may not have to leave at all, if you don't, you could repeat the same problem again.

Another example with a different problem. A woman who had trouble because her partner kept lying to her. After a while the relationship broke down, she left and found someone else, and it happened all over again.

The problem was not the men telling lies. The problem was she kept selecting and marrying men that were liars. Because she believed all men were liars, she was proving herself right. This was the real problem.

Robert Todd

UNLESS YOU CHANGE YOUR BELIEF SYSTEM YOU WILL KEEP GETTING THE SAME PROBLEM

REMOVING PAST LIFE PROBLEMS

THE CIRCLE TECHNIQUE

Over the years while counselling, I have developed and used different techniques. The most popular ones I referred to as the circle and the mirror techniques. I found these were suitable for different situations and seemed to be the most effective way to help.

The circle technique is used when people have several past lives with different characters that have a dramatic influence on their current life. Under hypnosis we bring each of the characters together at the end of a session in a circle, with her guide, so they can be individually dealt with giving understanding and forgiveness for the situations they created.

Then we use an energy from the guide and ask the client to have the energy flow from their heart into the next character in the circle through the crown chakra, down to their heart and then across to the crown chakra of the next person, this continues around the circle until it is fully connected. Next we ask the client to connect to the first person in the circle, talk about the situation that was created and offer them forgiveness for that event, then forgive herself for bringing that event and emotions into this life. Once they believe they have come to grips with that problem or situation they let that person go then move to the next person. Eventually we come around with the only one left being the guide and we thank them for their help and allow them to leave.

Having mentally dealt with the problem and forgiven them and themselves, this tends to stop that issue being dominant in their current life.

MIRROR TECHNIQUE

This technique is designed to help people who have lost confidence in the ability to solve problems and feel they are inadequate or cannot break out of the cycle they are in and feel unable to take steps to alter their situation.

While under a light hypnosis they are asked to stand a mirror in front of themselves. They are told, while looking in the mirror, they will see their image as they are now. I ask them to look at the way they display lack of confidence, and how their emotions are reflected in the image through body language.

Then they are directed to see into the image of the soul, to see the actual beauty of the soul, and to see how that image is showing confidence, success, in the body language. That image reflects confidence and the ability to interact with others, and all of the soul's potential.

I ask them to describe the differences they see. We now have the image reflecting the true person as they can be, and this is who they really are without any barriers.

Then we ask the image in the mirror to step out, turn around and meld into their current body. This allows the true self to be who they are. Then I ask them to take on all the characteristics within that image and to forgive themself for not being the person they really are. Once they have done this they again look into the mirror and see the reflection of the true self. Now they have adopted all of those characteristics into their life and can be who they were meant to be without any barriers.

I have found these methods to be very effective at changing people's perspective of themself.

Then Peter said I think we have talked enough today, let's talk about karma next time we meet.

> **ONCE YOU REMOVE YOUR BARRIERS YOU CAN BE THE TRUE SELF**

WE ASK FOR KARMIC LESSONS

Our next meeting was lunchtime and we sat at a small outdoor restaurant near his office and I started with a very simple question. Peter, you said we would talk about karma. What happens when we do something wrong, when our soul goes back home, how do we learn from that?

Let me give you a case example.

We often wonder how the other person felt. We decide to come down to earth and have a life where we can experience some of the same feelings, to understand and expand the soul. Let's say, rejection.

In a past life Mary had a baby with a married man outside her own marriage. She felt guilty, she also totally rejected the baby and although the baby died not long after birth, she wondered how it felt.

The baby dying early could have been a filler life, and is designed to increase the emotions she had about rejecting the baby. Children who die early, are sometimes incarnated so people can learn through the emotions of loss, and in her case, rejection. She knew the feeling of guilt, she wondered about the baby and the emotion of rejection. When she went back home and looked over her life, she realised how the child felt rejected.

Peter, are you saying because of that, she requested to learn about rejection in her next life.

Yes, she came to me because was she having problems with rejection, not knowing she had requested it. She also felt unworthy. Many of the goals she wanted to achieve, she would almost reach, then put a barrier in the way. She wanted to find out why she felt so inadequate and rejected.

I conducted a scene analysis, which gives me a good understanding of where her attitude is in life at the present. She was standing on the second floor of a house looking out of a glass window at a lake, with a hill in the background. This tells me because she was on the second floor, she was an observer of life at the present moment and not involved. The lake indicated that she wanted to be liked by people, but because she had the glass window in front of her, this was a barrier which was preventing her from moving forward. The hill in the distance shows that she has long-term objectives.

I guess Peter, you then did a past life regression to see what the blockage was and why she felt so inadequate?

Yes, and I will tell you step-by-step, the past life regression and what I found. Sometimes people repeat a lesson until learned.

REJECTED NOT WORTHY

Under a light hypnosis this is the session as it happened.

> Z. is Client   C. is Counsellor

C.   Going to go back in time to the very first time when you didn't feel worthy. What do you imagine is on your feet and anything else you can tell us?

Z.   Nothing, I have bare feet, I'm wearing loincloth I am a man and my name is Karuk age 35.

C.   How does Karuk feel?

Z.   Scared

C.   What's going on around him that's made him scared?

Z.   He's been banished by the tribe. He went against what the elders were saying. "There won't be excessive lack of food, and you can now survive on your own." He feels rejected and isolated.

C.   What decision did he make about himself and life at that time?

Z.   Keep quiet and go along with whatever they want.

C. Was he a good thinker and capable. Did he have confidence before this event took place?

Z. Yes, he still thinks he was right but afterwards maybe the tribe would survive.

C. What age did he die. Did he join any other tribe or live on his own?

Z. No, he was 80 when he died and he lived on his own.

C. Did he come out of that life thinking he should be quiet and be more of an observer?

Z. No, deciding to be true to himself, he gave up on interaction and enjoyed being on his own.

———————

Peter, what if she had learned all the aspects of rejection?

Thomas, if for example, Karuk had gone back to the tribe and apologised, they probably would have taken him in and he could have experienced some of the other concepts of rejection with the tribe. Unfortunately, he just stayed on his own and did not fully understand rejection by the time he died.

Peter, was there a reason he was isolated from the tribe at the age of 35?

I think it was probably because by that time he would have learned to be self-sufficient. If he had been banished any earlier, he may not have survived.

C. Now we're going to go to the next event or next life we need to know about. First let's look at what's on your feet and what clothes you are wearing?

Z. Pointy shoes, a nice blue dress sort of medieval time and I'm about 20, my name is Betty. I just broke up with my lover. He doesn't want me to speak, I mean I've got my own ideas.

C. And he doesn't like it, why not?

Z. Because it's not socially accepted and you can't have a woman smarter than him, according to him, that's not acceptable.

C. So he's trying to restrict you and that's why you broke up. Did you ever go with anyone else or did you stay entirely on your own?

Z. Never went with anyone else and yes, I stayed on my own the rest of my life.

C. Is that what you wanted?

Z. No. I wanted a man in a life where I felt I could discuss things openly, and someone with whom I felt equal.

C. Did you still express yourself when you considered yourself equal and what were the consequences of that?

Z. I was socially shunned and other men didn't want to be with me because of my knowledge and ability.

C.   Is that all we need to know about that life?

Z.   Yes, and I have two more we need to look at.

——————

Peter, in her first life she was a male and in this life female, again after the rejection, she just shut down and lived on her own.

That's correct Thomas, this happens quite often where people have a number of lives, sometimes male sometimes female trying to learn the same lesson.

——————

C.   Next life, what's on your feet and what are you wearing?

Z.   Boys school shoes long socks and dark grey clothes and I think I'm seven, my name is Boaz and I live in Holland.

C.   What year is it?

Z.   1697

C.   How are you feeling?

Z.   I am in trouble for speaking up, I'm going to the headmaster's office to be given the cane.

C.   What did you say?

Z. I was asking a question about astronomy and it was contrary to the current beliefs.

C. Were you a bit of a forward thinker when you were seven?

Z. Yes, I asked the teacher a question about what he was teaching and that was considered impertinent.

C. How did that affect Boaz?

Z. I just did not want to create any problems, I sort of became meek and mild. I developed throat problems. I still wanted to say things and ask questions but I felt I couldn't. I died in my sleep at about the age of 50 with breathing problems.

Peter, she did it again, this time the problem started at a very young age as a school boy, why?

Well Thomas, this is where people before the age of 13 have a problem which creates an attitude, so they can go through life and learn how to change them.

Oh Peter, she did not learn, she went through that whole life rejected and wouldn't speak up.

--- --- --- --- --- --- ---

C. Is that all we need to know and if so let's go to the fourth life. Tell me what's on your feet and what clothes are you wearing?

Z. Ski Boots and wearing grey clothes, I'm 25, my name is Hans and I seem to be by myself. Hans in fact follows his intuition and discovered he was rejected because the people he knew went by logic and did not agree with him.

C. I don't think we need to know much about this life as you seem to have done the same thing, again gone through life on your own.

Peter, she has learned four different ways to be rejected, and she has not used her free-will to change her attitude.

Current Life

C. Now I want to go to this life and find out why you felt rejected so we can connect what is causing your problem at this time.

Z. I am barefoot and we just had a lot of rain and it is muddy. I am four years old, played in the mud and I'm all covered with mud and my grandmother came and cleaned everything up and she sat us down and got us to do some writing. She gave my cousin five dollars and she didn't give me anything.

C. So how do you feel about that?

Z. Terrible grandmother said, I should be able to write but I'm four years old and I hadn't been taught.

C. So why did that make you isolate yourself and put up a barrier?

Z. Because I was her granddaughter and she was only a cousin and she was six and got money (tears and crying) it was at that.

C. It was, you felt rejected because you're different, can you understand that feeling?

Z. Yes, couldn't do it, you have to work very hard to be happy, otherwise you wouldn't get any money. Being close to someone doesn't count.

C. So you stop getting close to people, because you were close to grandma, but it didn't do anything for you. She didn't give you any money, yet your cousin was not close at all and she got money. So being close to anybody didn't do anything for you. So, is that when you shut off?

Z. Yes

— — — — — — —

Peter is this again before the age of 13 she has an attitude set up?

I would say so Thomas, once again, she unfortunately failed to change.

C.   Now I want you to look at the four lives. There was an isolation point in each life. They had the intelligence and the ability to ask questions and each time they did this there was rejection.

Now we must ask why this rejection had taken place. Were you just starting to learn about rejection as a soul, was that the quest you came down to understand. Ask your guide was there a previous time in a previous life where you rejected something or someone, what was the reason that you needed to learn this lesson?

Z.   Because in a previous life I had a baby and I was pushing it away, I didn't want it. It was before all of these lives.

C.   Did you have other children. What is the story regarding this baby. Why did you reject it?

Z.   It wasn't with my husband. I had it with a married man, but it didn't live, died not long after birth.

C.   So, you've chosen four karmic lives to teach you about rejection.

SUMMARY

Interesting because she had four lives. Karuk the Indian in a desert, who was rejected at the age of 35 mainly because he spoke up against the elders.

The second one was Betty who broke up with her boyfriend, because she was more intelligent and he felt that would be bad for society purposes, and he also had other friends reject her because she may influence the wives of his friends.

The next was young Boaz who asked questions in school and was caned because he asked about astrology which was against the beliefs at that time.

The final was Hans and he was in fact following his intuition and was rejected because he was with people who went by logic and did not agree.

When we asked why she was going through the rejection process she said she had had a baby which she had rejected because it was an affair with a married man. Then before she came back to earth, she asked to have lives to learn about rejection and in this life with her grandmother, she is still repeating rejection until she learns.

All this because she asked if she could understand rejection.

Karma is a fascinating thing

— — — — — — —

Robert Todd

Peter, what happened at the end of the session?

That was interesting Thomas, we went back and looked at her scene. She was now standing on the ground floor at an open front door of the house. Showing that we had removed the barrier that was preventing her achieving what she wanted. She is now aware and can change her attitude and approach and live a happy life overcoming rejection.

KARMA IS A FASCINATING THING

SEPARATION AND REJECTION

This client was put under a light hypnosis and this is the session as it happened.

K. is Client   C. is Counsellor

Life 1

C. What do you see? Describe in detail what's on your feet, your clothes and anything else that comes to mind.

K. I'm wearing woolly shoes and clothes I am about 20, I have a spear and I think hunting bison.

C. What is his name?

K. Grorl

C. You will know everything he knows and you will also feel his emotions. How do you feel?

K. Scared

C. What are you scared of?

K. Men will see me.

C. Why are you scared of the men?

K. I'm supposed to be a man, it's a ritual.

C. Do you have to kill a bison to prove you are a man? What's the fear of killing it?

K. I don't want to kill it, I'm not really a strong man and I have trouble, I'm not really tough.

C. Why did you choose to come down into this life and have the feeling of not being manly enough, what was your family upbringing like?

K. My mother is very timid, my father is not really strong either.

C. So, move forward and see if you actually killed the bison?

K. No, I found a deer that was much easier.

C. How did the tribe feel about that?

K. I felt humiliated, because that was all I could get.

C. Is there any more we need to know about that?

K. No

C. Go to your next area of importance.

———————

Peter, was there a reason that she came down so timid, with parents who were not really that strong?

When we come down, we choose the parents that will most help us achieve the goals we set. I was not sure at this stage why that was happening but we found out later in the session.

— — — — — — —

Life 2

K. I have boots on my feet, a white shirt and brown pants. I am still a man and I'm very handsome, short brown curly hair, white skin and I have a quill in my hand. I am about 26 years old, single, my name is Jeremy. This is prior to when I was Grorl, the year is 1635.

C. Now you will know everything Jeremy is feeling and thinking at the age of 26, holding a quill.

K. Romantic.

C. What have you been doing with this quill?

K. Writing poetry.

C. Is this the life that set you up to have that feeling of weakness in the previous life we discussed. Was it you didn't have to get out into the real world, you were wealthy.

K. Well off, big house out in the country, long way from the road and had a very quiet life.

C. What did your parents do to earn all this money?

K. We had a big property, big fields and people working out in the fields for us.

C. Did you take over from what your father was doing?

K   He was working till he was 80 and I was just a poet. My mum was very nice, she was protecting me. My Poppa was very very angry, he was an arrogant fool.

C. Take us forward in time and tell me what went on in your life, let's say at the age of 40.

K   I'm in Poppa's room.

C. What does your Poppa think of you now?

K   My Poppa threw me out, he thinks I am lazy

C. Did you ever get married?

K   No.

C. Let's go through till the end of your life, what age did you die?

K   I died at the age of 64 and I was very poor and I haven't been eating probably.

C. Do we need to know any more about that and if not, do we need to go to a third life?

— — — — — — —

Peter, that explains why Grorl had such a meek and mild attitude, he was a poet in his previous life. So this life was affecting the one we first talked about. Do you sometimes get lives out of order.

Yes Thomas, because it depends on the question I ask and the importance of the life they describe. This is where it can be confusing sometimes.

─ ─ ─ ─ ─ ─ ─

Life 3

K.   Yes, there is an old bent over woman named Isabel. She is like an old witch, she has black clothes and seems as if she only sneaks out at night and she's afraid of money.

C.   How did she survive if she is afraid of the money?

K.   She makes potions for pretty girls, love potions. There is a 20-year-old girl and she is giving her a potion to treat the boy she wants.

C.   Does she believe her potions work because of the chemicals or is it just in the mind?

K.   She believes it's the chemicals. She feels alone and misunderstood but she heals herself with her herbs and plants. She was very happy when she was young, she was very outgoing.

C.   So what changed that?

K   Someone got shipwrecked and she lost the love of her life.

C.   Do we need to know any more about the shipwreck, or this life and what happened?

K.   No

———————

So Peter, she turned the loss of love into a desire to help others achieve what she did not have.

Yes this often happens, maybe she needed to learn to be stronger and not so sheltered.

———————

Life 4

K.   This time I have gold slippers and gold shoes and have my hair done and beads around a beautiful white gown, I am 35 and my name is Caren or Carin

C.   What's going on around you?

K.   There's a man there, Philip and we are together. We are married, very rich and we are in France 1730.

C.   What's happening in your life and how do you feel about life?

K.   I have 2 children and a nanny who looks after them. I'm not very close to them and I'm lonely because we live out in the country again.

C.   Did your husband make the money or did he inherit the money?

K.   It's all his and his mother's money. She lives with us and he's very close to his mother.

C.   What is the relationship with your husband?

K.   It's a comfortable relationship, not romantic love, a marriage of convenience. We met at a party and I enjoy parties with soldiers and people in high up positions but that part of my life is gone, no more parties.

C.   What are you wishing for?

K.   Change. When I got to 40 or 50 the relationship is changed. We were much more distant, then I get older and more matronly. I don't know where he is now, he's gone somewhere, mum still here and the children have gone.

C.   Is this all we need to know is there something particular we should look at?

K.   No

— — — — — —

Peter, that's strange. She had two children and had a very awkward relationship with them because they had a nanny, her husband became estranged and she just lived with the mother-in-law who had all the money.

Yes she has certainly had a variety over the lives we have seen so far, interesting. I guess they tied together somehow. Let's see what the next one brings.

— — — — — — —

Life 5

K. In my next life I'm wearing black shoes and I'm a man with a suit on and a hat, got no money, this is the 1900's and my name is Jimmy. I am well liked and feel good. I think I'm dark skinned and about 30, maybe 35. I am a bit of a rogue, and I work for a boss man. I organise games, boxing games and betting.

C. What is the most important thing about this life?

K. Shame he got mixed up with a married woman, the boss's daughter. She got a bit serious but he wasn't and because of the relationship he got shot by the big boss. Ended up in hospital and is not so happy anymore in his life. He can't go back into that old life and he became a drifter, he moves to a small town and becomes an alcoholic and dies.

C. Now I want to summarise what we've got so we are going back to Jeremy around 1635. He started off fairly well in life as a poet then his father kicked him out at 43 and he ended up very lonely and on his own. What was the lesson in that life?

K. He had to learn about selfishness.

C. Selfishness caused him to end up dying poor and not in a good condition. Did he take the characteristics of Jeremy when he came into the life of Grorl. Is this why he was scared, he did not feel like a man and chose a mother who was a bit timid, as he hadn't handled it previously when he was Jeremy, can you see the connection?

K. Yes

C. Did his father say he couldn't stand up for himself when he was Jeremy and this is why he threw him out and he came back in his next life trying to fix that problem as Grorl and ended up very timid and scared. The next one to come through was 1730, Caren, who came down as a woman to find out what her mother was doing and why. We can see if Caren had money, she would be okay and she didn't care much about the children and figured if she had the money she would be okay.

K. I can see the connection because Jeremy had the money and lost it. Caren needed the money to feel secure. Then she came back as a woman named Isabel.

C. Can you see how Isabel had no money and she came down to try and understand about love. She lost her love, then tried to help other people find the love that she never really had because she lost it in a shipwreck. Then she came down as Jimmy in the 1900s. He came down strong, like the boxers and the boss, and he had no money. Then he was chased by the boss's daughter and was shot. So each time you started out okay and then got lost, is that what you are learning.

K.   Yes

C.   First of all, we have Jeremy who was lazy and unsure of himself, poetry was most important and he lost his manhood and his strength. Can you see how he became uncertain and money became scarce in his life. What is the most important aspect of his life that we need to bring into this life.

K.   To be creative but make sure we do not become arrogant.

C.   Now we look at Grorl he was trying to be a man but he chose to be timid which caused the problems in his life. Who is the mum of that life in this life?

K.   It's my mum she is with me again.

C.   Has she change from that life?

K.   No, she is the same.

This case study shows over many lifetimes, we will have different personalities and different experiences, which give us either strengths or weaknesses. We will also find there are times where one life effects another, although may not be the direct next life. It could be a life in the future or we can go back and work on the past life's problems. Also, you will notice we can have different countries, and sometimes male and sometimes female, with different skin colours, be in a society where they fit in or are rejected. Sometimes they will have long lives sometimes short lives, depending on the problem they are trying to solve.

HOW ONE LIFE CAN AFFECT CURRENT LIVES

Thomas, I remember the story about the woman who, in a past life was in charge of a gladiator and after she ordered him to the arena, he was killed.

Also in another previous life she was a pilot in the Second World War. She was ordered by someone else to fly a dangerous mission where she was injured seriously and others died. This was the event that caused her fear of flying in this lifetime.

Now in this life she has to order herself to fly home. This, of course, is the karmic turnaround. She is not ordering someone else, she is ordering herself to fly.

So Peter, the experience with the gladiator and second world war is causing her to be scared.

That is correct Thomas, you can now see how one or more lives can be affected by events from previous lives.

Peter, do you have other examples of people who have brought forward karma from previous lives which cause problems in their current life.

Thomas, I have so many examples. In fact I worked in the area of phobias and they were often caused by events in previous lives. However, some phobias are caused by events in this life. Remember many of these events prior to the age of 13, were set up before coming to earth, to remind them of the problem they need to solve.

The next case is one where a member of the family had a phobia he needed to solve and the whole family reincarnated together to solve many of their relationship problems.

FAMILIES CAN REINCARNATE AS A GROUP

TO SOLVE A NUMBER OF PROBLEMS

Peter, there was a case study in your previous book. It was case study number 16 and was a story of Andrew. Can you explain it for me in far more detail?

Okay Thomas, I will keep Andrew's name. I will also name the other characters just so it is easier to follow.

This case is very fascinating, it shows how someone can live parallel lives. Andrew lived one life as a senator. His second life at the same time was the son of a tribal leader of a small village. His mother in the same life was a male and member of the Senate.

These two groups were about to go to war against each other. He had a life on each side of the upcoming war. In both cases he was against the war, and his parents were in favour of the war for different reasons.

When he starts his story, he says he has different clothes on the left and right side of his body. This was confusing until my guide told me he was describing parallel lives.

The universe is very clever as to how it attempts to solve problems. It is quite common for a husband and wife to come to earth in several lives in different roles till they learn to solve all situations. When they went to the afterlife, they would be taught how to handle it differently. Then they come down to test what they have learned and how to put the solution into effect.

Andrew came to me with a fear of fountains. If he went into a park where there was a fountain, he would have a panic attack.

I took Andrew back to a life where he was a senator in Rome.

His father (named Sam) was also a Senator. His father wanted to go to war against a small village, so he could get more money from them in the form of land tax and cattle tax.

Andrew also had a younger brother (named Jack) and his brother would do anything to get his father's attention.

The village leader (named John) did not want to go to war but is determined to defend his village and not pay any taxes.

The village leaders son (named Bill) was not happy about going to war but he really had no alternative. He was the second part of Andrews soul.

Andrew was against the war and Sam his father was not at all happy because Andrew could influence the Senate and stop the war and therefore the income.

So the senator, Sam, conspired with his youngest son Jack to have Andrew killed. Jack, Andrew's younger brother, did this by stabbing Andrew in the back and drowning him in a fountain. This is where Andrew's fear of fountains in this life, was created.

They did go to war and the senator named Sam won the war.

During the fighting the village leader's son named Bill was killed.

So Peter, all that happened in a past life. So how does that affect this life?

Thomas, this is where it becomes complicated.

LETS MOVE TO THIS LIFE

Life And What Happens When We Die

In this cycle of reincarnation, the senator Sam reincarnated as a woman (named Samantha) and she had two sons Jack and Andrew.

Now she married the village leader, who reincarnated as a man, John.

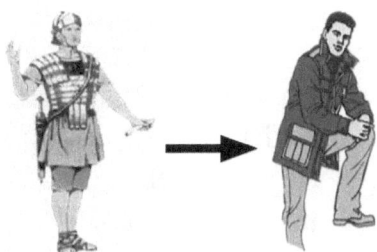

Jack was the youngest in the previous life and now becomes the oldest in this life.

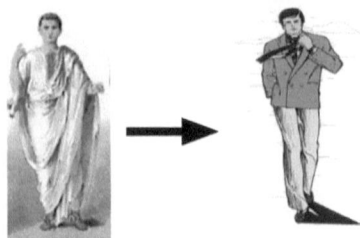

Andrew the oldest in the previous life, now becomes the youngest in this life.

Let's look at what happens to them in this life caused by the events of the last life.

Because Samantha had Andrew killed in the last life she had to come back as a woman and give him back the life she took. She went to war for power and money. Yet in this life as a woman born in the 1940s life was different. Married women tended to stay at home and look after the family, and money was a problem. Now she had to make a choice between money and family.

In the last life he lost the war, and became subservient to the senator, now as Samantha is his wife, he must try to be much stronger. He was her enemy in one life and now married in this life. Unfortunately, he has not fully learnt that lesson and Samantha tends to still be in charge.

The younger brother in the previous life is now the oldest brother. Remember he killed his older brother Andrew in the previous life, and now protects his younger brother in this life to make up for what he did in the last life.

It is all good Peter, what happened to Andrew?

Well Andrew went on to a much easier life where he no longer was afraid of fountains, as he realised it is not likely that he is going to be stabbed in the back and drowned in a fountain in this lifetime, especially by his brother who is now protecting him.

SHUT DOWN TO LOVE

When Jenny, 24 years old, came to me she described how she sits in a coffee shop looking at people who were pretending they were happy. She would like to find a relationship but not a dishonest one like them. She could not find a close relationship.

This went back to when she was seven years old and her brother was diagnosed with a tumour in his chest. She decided she did not want to lose her brother because she relied on him. He was much older than her. At that point she turned herself off because she did not want to lose love. This is why she was sitting in the coffee shop watching people and deciding if they were real or fakes and identify those who were positive and those who were not.

Let's look at the actual case as it progressed.

Z. is Client   C. is Counsellor

C.   Just relax, you have been an observer of life since you shut down. Now going back to the original cause of the problem, I want you to look back into the past and you will see a person, can you tell me what their name is?

Z.   I am in a café sitting with someone. It's a male, it's my brother, my name is Jenny and I am on holidays. The people around me are very nice upper-class, I'm not like these people but I would like to be. Like the people walking past, I want to have what they have, but not be like they are.

C. So what's stopping you being like that?

Z. I'm not always happy, I'm worrying about where I'm going, I worry about friends and my brother because he is not well. I don't think he's telling me everything.

C. How does that affect your life?

Z. He's happy, I'm happy.

C. Why do you have to have your brother happy to make you happy? We are going to go back in time as to why your brother has to be happy, before you can be happy. Tell me what's on your feet?

Z. Standing in water, I have black shorts and a black top. I am seven and my brother is 14 he has a tumour in his chest. I love him and he is my protector, I don't want him to go, he is going to die.

C. Who told you that?

Z. Nobody it's just what happens.

C. What decision are you making about yourself and life at this point in time?

Z. I want to protect him, I want to be happy but I can't, so I don't want anybody in my life. I don't want to get close to anybody because I might lose them.

C. Did your brother die from the tumour?

Z. Yes, he died at age 22 and I was 15 I think.

C. What decision did you make about life at that time?

Z. That's life. I want to be really happy.

C. That's really hard when you are seven and you get that information about your brother. You made the decision to shut yourself off and not go with anyone because you didn't want to lose them. You shut down yourself so you would not suffer the pain of losing someone.

At this stage I used the mirror technique.

Now can you see that when anybody looks at you they will see that love, the real you, beautiful and loving as you are.

Z. Yes

C. Now you never need to go back into your shell. You can now move forward freely in life without fear. When you look at someone else, you will know and see the love within them. You will also be able to see the falseness within people, like you did when you were sitting at that restaurant. You will recognise the truth within each person you meet, so you can share your love freely and find your soulmate.

> Now we're going to go back to that scene in the coffee shop. As you look around you will be able to see the truth, those that are really happy, and those that are not, can you see that?

Z.   Yes

C.   We have taken away all the blockages to life. You will feel different, you will be free, more relaxed and able to become friends with other trusting people, and I'm sure you will find yourself a wonderful partner when the time is right. How do you feel?

Z.   I feel happy and free and a lot more confident about understanding people, thank you.

Thomas, I think it would be better if we stop here and have our next meeting in about a week.

WOULD NOT CROSS OVER

Peter had another conference to attend and suggested I meet him for lunch at the hotel after his talk, which would be about 2.30pm and we can spend some time before he went home. I asked him is it true that some people hang around after they die and don't go into the light?

Sometimes people will not cross over because they do not feel they have completed everything they wanted to achieve in their life. Maybe they died early or they feel an obligation to someone they want to help and maintain a relationship.

This is a case where the mother would not cross over because she wanted to help her daughter. Unfortunately, her connection to her daughter was creating problems. The daughter felt she could feel her mother with her all the time. When it came to making decisions, it was difficult as she was continually thinking she had to please her mother, not herself.

I put her under a light hypnosis.

X. is Client   C. Is Counsellor

C. Who is your guide?

X. Mother, but I'm having trouble understanding her. I know she is with me and watching me whenever I try to make a decision.

C.   Check, has she gone into the light?

X.   No

C.   Tell her you want her to do a favour for you. Tell her she needs to go into the light and she will find it much easier to contact you at any time.

X.   She doesn't want to go. She doesn't want to leave me.

C.   Tell her it will be a long time before you are together. If she goes, all will be added unto her. All the things she wants will be available to her.

X.   She has decided to go. She's gone into the light. I can't feel her anymore.

C.   That's okay, that's okay. Now a new guide will come out of the light.

X.   It's grandma!

C.   Ask your grandma did she just meet your mother?

X.   Yes! and they're both so happy.

C.   Now they are together, ask your grandma to ask your mum to also come out.

X.   Yes, mum is now with her, I can see them both.

C.   Now they can both help you and you can talk to them whenever you want. Ask your mum how she felt when she went into the light?

X. She felt great love, and is happy.

C. Tell her you want to make decisions on your own and see what she says.

X. She now knows that she shouldn't have stayed around all the time and that I have my own life to live.

**BUT SEEK FIRST
THE KINGDOM OF GOD
AND HIS RIGHTEOUSNESS
AND
ALL THESE THINGS WILL
BE ADDED UNTO YOU**

PERSONALITY

People ask about personality. We often reincarnate with the same people or partners. When two people, husband and wife, have different sessions, what often happens is that the person under hypnosis say their partner's personality was the same personality they had in a previous life.

Other questions often asked are why do two children in the same family have different personalities. Some say their children are nothing like they are. Others say something like, one of my children is like my husband or one is like my wife.

This could be because before we come down, we pick our parents and possibly pick the personalities, DNA and knowledge that enable us to achieve the solutions to our current problems. Also, we pick parents with the personality we want so we feel comfortable, indicating that personality is our choice and can flow through from life to life.

I have had many cases where this has shown to be true.

CONVERSATION ABOUT UNDERSTANDING GOD

This gentleman came to me with a problem, he said he was having difficulty making decisions. He did not know what he wanted to achieve in life and seemed hesitant to move ahead with anything. It's as if he was totally unable to make a firm decision as to what way he should go. He had had a lot of traumas in his life and had turned to religion in an attempt to solve his problem.

He doesn't understand God, yet he said he is a born again Christian. He lost a brother in a motorbike accident; his other brother was murdered and his mother died of cancer when she was 56. He thinks God is unfair because of these situations and now he does not know what to do with his life. I think this is why he became a born again Christian. I also think this is stopping him making decisions in case he does not please God.

Even under hypnosis he could not answer the questions I asked. I had not struck this before so for the first time I made the decision to talk and present a decision I thought may help. It seemed to have the desired effect.

Y. is Client   C. Is Counsellor

C. Why are you a born again Christian if you don't understand God? Are you just trying to please God so you get to Heaven? Is it so if you die you hope you go to Heaven, is that a hope or a reality?

Y. Pretty sure about that I'm a Pentecostal Christian.

C. That doesn't seem to make you understand what God is doing or why.

I think you are just hoping you please God and you don't know how. You're hoping in the end you will make heaven.

Y. I just want to please him, I think that's what I should do.

C. Is he pleasing you? You don't understand him.

Y. I'm just trying to understand.

C. You say you don't know your direction. You shut off your emotions and you're not game to do anything in case it's wrong.

You're thinking, I've got to be good and I've got to say I am a born again Christian. I've got to do the right thing to please him, yet you believe he's unfair.

While ever you hold that belief you will always see him as unfair, because God only ever does what you believe. He makes no judgement with unconditional love and gives you what you ask for.

No judgement, so whatever you believe he is, he will be. If you don't understand him, then he can't explain to you who he truly is. He cannot give you the answers and there is logic in what has happened.

There is a reason for what has happened and because your mind is the way it is, you will never understand.

The reason you are shut down is because it's too scary.

We will have to move away from human logic. Look for understanding behind these events. We have to look at the universal purpose and see why things happen, before you can ever understand God.

We often get caught up in human logic and emotions, which cloud our true perception as to God's purpose.

It can be too scary and until we release the emotions, all it does is shut us down and then we get to a point we don't know our direction.

I have a very strong belief in God and what he does. The point is, what at this time does God want from you? Like any father he would want his son to succeed, what do you have to give him to reach your full potential?

Y. I just think he likes to see people reach their full potential.

C. Do you know what he wants from you? Absolutely nothing. There is no judgement, doubt or uncertainty or conditional love.

If you know your Bible you'll know when the Prodigal son came home, his son said "father I have sinned" and his father said, in modern terms, "let's forget all that rubbish and let's all have a party". Because as far as God is concerned you are already perfect.

So what does God want to give you. The Bible says, he who is great among you let him serve. So who do you think is the great?

Y.   God and Jesus

C.   I was referring to people on earth. As you know Jesus came to save the Jews, unfortunately they did not recognise him as their leader. The disciples and gentiles who call themselves Christians recognise him as the Trinity, Father Son and Holy Spirit. We also know Jesus died on the cross for the Christians who believed and accepted his sacrifice. God has accepted us and applied the Bible statement, ask and you will receive. God wants you to ask for the things you want, without fear, so you live a happy beautiful secure life full and love.

You are afraid that if you ask for something, he may not like it and you want to please him so you get to heaven. You have been taught by your religion if you're good, you might make it.

Let's look at your life, your mother didn't die because God took her. When your mum got cancer, what did the doctor say. Did he say she had six or twelve months to live? If she accepts that and it becomes part of her belief system, then God grants that decision and it will become reality.

God tells us to ask in a very particular way, *ask as if it already is.*

You visualise what you do want and you visualise it *as if it already is*, for what you can see and believe becomes reality.

When you allow your emotions to get total control of your belief system and you believe that God is unfair, then that becomes your reality.

Our language and our attitude to all things creates our future and you at the moment, have difficulty making up your mind.

You say, I can't make a decision, then that will become part of your life, because you asked for it.

Then God has trouble getting through to you, even to give the things you do want, because your belief system is stopping it.

Whatever decision you make is okay, believe in yourself and your ability, all things are available for you.

When your brothers and mother died, you shut off your emotions. Then you say, I don't understand why she died, then God can't get through.

Stop worrying, God loves you and he wants you to have the things you want in life. So go out and enjoy life. Make whatever decision with love for yourself and others and God will help you, then be the true born again Christian you are and enjoy life. Do you understand and is it okay with you? Are you going to trust God from now on and tell him what you want, instead of being scared. Give him unconditional trust.

Y.   Yes, thanks. You are right, I was scared of making a mistake. Thank you, thank you, I need to change my belief system and enjoy life with God's help.

GOD LOVES ALL OF US AND WANTS US TO BE WITH HIM

THE SUBJECT RACISM

This world is designed as a school. We come here to learn to grow and understand the emotion of fear. When it comes to being racist this is a very important subject.

We may dislike a person but we should never dislike a race. In their race there are many different people, and many races from different countries on this earth. All of them have a purpose, all of them are designed to help us learn and grow.

Be careful how you judge others because when you go back you will judge yourself by those same standards.

Over many lifetimes you have reincarnated into different countries, different cultures, different families, you have probably taken on many roles. You may have been Atlantean or Arabians, early American Indians, Africans, English, Russian, Irish, or any other nationality you can think of. You may have been black, white, yellow, or any mixture that is available.

You may have been in a religion that had 24 Gods, one God or you may have been Buddhist, Islamic, Atheist, Christian or again any other religious group. The universe always provides different situations and nationalities to give us greater learning of different cultures and backgrounds, to teach you certain lessons.

If there are individuals who you are not happy with, that is ok, but might I suggest you ask yourself why, and maybe learn to understand their situation, because in the end you will be judged by yourself, relative to your attitude to others.

If you have created situations and problems for a particular race or group of people, you could very well reincarnate into that group so you understand exactly what they're going through.

You will notice in this book people change from male to female and also to different nationalities. At some stage in your reincarnation history over many lifetimes you may have been, as I said, any other nationality that has existed on earth.

Thomas, I have meetings all next week, can we make our next meeting in about two weeks. I will contact you and let you know where and when.

IN PREVIOUS LIVES YOU MAY HAVE BEEN MALE, FEMALE, BLACK, WHITE, OR ANY OTHER SKIN COLOUR

HOW KARMA AFFECTS OUR LIVES

Peter rang me and the next meeting was held in his office. When I arrived his secretary brought us coffee and cake which created a good atmosphere, then Peter started talking about karma and its effects.

The problem stated by the client before hypnosis was that she continually picks people with whom she was not emotionally involved. She needs to understand why she picked her particular husband.

Z. is Client   C. is Counsellor

Current Life

C.   What is on your feet and anything else that you can tell me about what's going on around you now?

Z.   Bare feet, a nappy, I am two years old named Heather

C.   How are you feeling Heather?

Z.   Sad nobody came to help me.

C.   Why do you need help?

Z.   He's beating me, dad beating me.

C. What decisions are you making about the world while your dad is beating you?

Z. I am alone and he won't let them come.

C. Will you ask your guide, do we need to know any more about that scene?

Z. No, I was two and dad said I wouldn't do what I was told.

C. Will you now go to the next scene. Your guide wants us to be aware of why you chose a father who would beat you, where are you now?

— — — — — — —

Past Life 2

Z. I am wearing sandals and stripey clothes, I'm a man 30 years old, my name is Joseph.

C. Where are you?

Z. I am in a market looking for something.

C. How are you feeling?

Z. Lonely

C. Do you have any family?

Z. A little girl, my wife died at 26 years old.

C. Tell me about the little girl?

Z. She is four and hangs onto my mundu most of the time. I feel remote from the little girl and she is there all the time, I don't get a break. I am a shopkeeper and she is just there all the time (starts crying) I love her and I miss my wife.

C. It's okay, let's go forward a few years to the next important point in your life.

Z. It's a wedding, my daughter's wedding.

C. How old are you now and how do you feel about the wedding?

Z. 50 and sad and lonely.

C. You lost your wife and now you're losing your little girl, that's hard. Was she happily married and well looked after?

Z. Yes

C. Do we need to know any more about that time.

Z. I died at the age of 54, never remarried because I didn't think I could stand any more pain, and left my daughter some money to help her.

— — — — — — —

Past Life 1

C. So, let's move on to the next important point we need to know about. What's on your feet and how do you feel and what's going on around you?

Z. My name is Jecenta, I've got black shoes, I have on a dress with a lot of old gold and silver. I am very angry.

C. Why are you angry?

Z. My servants won't do what they're told, I get cranky because I can't find my things and I have to blame someone and I get cranky with them. They get sent to the kitchen and that's not a nice place to work.

C. What is really hurting you and making you so angry that you have to take it out on someone else?

Z. I have to make all the decisions by myself - I am the Queen. I have to make all the decisions for the country.

C. And it's too much for you, are you on your own with no king?

Z. He died, he fell off his horse. I'm on my own, lonely, it's all too hard.

SUMMARY

C. If we look at what happened, when you were the Queen you are overwhelmed. Your next life you came back as a man running a shop, Joseph, and you had one child because you wanted a simple life. This time you lost your wife, so you would see what it was like but it wasn't so simple. In the previous life you were Queen who lost her king and it wasn't simple either and you took your frustration out on everyone even though they were probably not in the wrong.

This life you came back as the two-year-old who was getting beaten because you wouldn't do what you were told. Isn't that the same as the Queen with her servants? Maybe your father was taking out his frustration on you. Can you see how your father was transferring his anger by taking it out on you.

Is this when you made the decision not to be emotionally involved and not to get into a complicated life. Can you see why the Queen got so angry, can you forgive the her for that?

Z.   Yes. She was just overwhelmed.

C.   Can you understand your father was overwhelmed and he was taking it out on you and you understand now how the servants felt. They could not do anything, the same as a two-year-old could not do anything. Do you understand now your servant's frustration and your father's frustration and can you forgive him and understand two very hard lessons you have learnt?

Z.   Yes, it is very hard but I can see why and what was happening and it was a very hard lesson to go through.

C.   This is what we call karma and it can certainly be very difficult but remember you chose it. Now you have to go beyond it and move on with your life once you forgive your father and show compassion for your servants. It shows you have learnt your lesson. So you can you tell the Queen you love her and you forgive her. Tell your father you love him and forgive him for the experience you chose.

Z.   Now that I understand, dad I can forgive you and I love you and the Queen. I understand what you were going through, I love you and I forgive you.

C.   Now I want you to go to the life where you were Joseph, where you lost your wife and your daughter got married and the feeling of loneliness and separation. You decided you would not get involved again because of the feeling of loss. This is not something you want in this life. You had a lesson that you do not want to be on your own. So, thank him for the experience and tell him you love him and you understand and you will make sure you are not alone in this life.

Z.   Thank you, Joseph, for that information and experience. I love you and I will certainly make sure I do not experience it in this lifetime.

I then used the mirror technique to bring love, freedom and understanding into her physical self.

LOST HERSELF

In this case, Lynn came to me and said her life was not good and she felt she was not worthy of anything better. It is typical where a person repeats the emotions of a previous life in the current life. Usually, it is prior to the age of 15. It is to teach them to move beyond those types of emotions and in her case, it happened when she was six years old.

Z. is Client   C. is Counsellor

C. You are going into a white cloud and as you look around, you will see a scene. I want you to tell me exactly what's going on, for example what's on your feet and the clothes you are wearing.

— — — — — — —

Current Life

Z. Bare feet, jeans, white T-shirt, aged 15. My name is Lynn.

C. What's going on around you?

Z. Mum and my stepfather are awful.

C. What decision did you make about life at this time and how are you feeling?

Z. I didn't want this kind of life. A lot of fear. I want to run away.

C. We are going to ask you why you chose this type of life, why you chose those parents. We are going to go back in time to find out why. Tell me what's on your feet and any other information you may have?

— — — — — — —

Past Life

Z. Sandals, draping clothes, creamy white not real clean. My name is Sarah, 20 years old and I am very sad.

In a lot of pain in my heart (started to cry) there are people around me fighting with swords, my partner got killed.

C. Did you ever find another partner?

Z. No. Not after my lover was killed. I didn't deserve any more.

C. How old were you when you died?

Z. 40.

C. I think that's all we need to know so let's go to another lifetime. Tell me what's on your feet and anything else you can describe?

— — — — — — —

Current Life

Z. Shoes, a check dress, my name is Lynn, I am six years old and it is my party, I am happy. I can't find dad and now I feel sad.

C. Tell me if you are feeling the same type of sadness as when you were Sarah and she lost her partner?

Z. Yes

C. When you got that feeling do you feel you don't deserve anything else?

Z. Very tired, it goes straight to my heart and takes it away.

C. We are going back into the cloud. I want you to stand Sarah in front of you. I want you to bring a light from the cloud into Sarah's crown chakra then to her heart and then across into yours. I want you to allow the love and understanding to flow between you and Sarah and I want you to understand that Sarah made a decision when she lost her lover that she didn't deserve any more.

Was that really right for her that she lived the rest of her life till she was 40, punishing herself for that experience. She ground that so much into her soul that when you came into this life, you brought it with you again. Can you understand how she made that decision and it's come forward to you.

Z. Yes, she got a rough deal.

C. Can you forgive her for that decision and tell her she was more worthy than all of that. It's just that she restricted herself because of the strong love she had for her boyfriend.

Explain to her that you brought that into this lifetime and you no longer need it. You understand the loneliness she went through, but you don't need it anymore in this lifetime. I want you to ask her for one piece of advice for this lifetime.

Z. Don't be afraid.

C. Can you send her love and thank her for that?

Z. Thank you and I love you.

C. Now I want you to go and look at the little girl at the party and see the excitement she had, then the sadness when she realised her dad was not there. Understand that took you right back to Sarah and the sadness she had in that life and the same decision you made then came back again. Can you forgive yourself for making that decision and give yourself love.

Z. Yes, I forgive myself and I certainly give a lot of love to the little girl, me.

C. We don't need that decision in your life anymore and now I want you to bring an image of yourself when you were Lynn at 15, and you were there with your mum and your stepfather. You wanted to run away and they were trying to tell you that you didn't need your first dad and you could stand on your own at 15?

It was a safe world and you could move beyond the point of loneliness and I'm not worthy. When you look at your family you could see that they were not worthy and that you are worthy of much more than that. Can you see that and understand your decision. Now I want you to give love to yourself when you were 15 and thank her for the feelings she had and it is okay to move on.

Z.   Yes

Once again I used the mirror technique to instil the new feelings and emotions and strength in her.

WHEN PEOPLE LOSE SOMEONE THEY LOVE THEY CAN SHUT DOWN

FIGHT TO THE DEATH

Z. is Client   C. is Counsellor

C. We want to go back in time to find out why you bring cycles of good and bad into your life. We always have a reason. We are the cause, we want to know the true cause. Ask your guide the base reason why it exists.

Tell me anything that comes to your mind?

Z. I see a caveman, he's fighting.

C. What is he fighting about or for?

Z. He wants to protect his cave, his home, it's where he has always lived (starts crying). He wants to protect his home but the other person wants it, he is bigger and stronger, yet I killed him.

C. How does that make him feel and what decision did he make about life?

Z. Life sucks. I didn't like it but it's what you have to do. (Still crying)

C. Did this event cause you to think that every time you get something, someone else wants it and wants to take it from you. Have you had this for many lives. You don't want to be angry, is it your fault or theirs?

Z. It just is (still crying)

C. Is this the only life where this has happened or are there other lives?

Z. There is Genie, in the forest, she just wanted to get some food, she was starving. She couldn't breathe and she died.

C. Are there any other lives, ask your guide?

Z. I am a knight on a horse, just come back from the Crusades. I went to fight the war and I was killing people and I didn't like to do that, so I refused and was called a traitor and I was to be executed for that.

C. How did he feel about the fact he will be killed because he wouldn't kill?

Z. It's just the way it is. It's always a fight to the death.

C. So he's going to be beheaded, how does he feel?

Z. Happy, it's just the way it is.

C. I just want to concentrate on the three lives, the first one when you were fighting to protect your cave, no matter what, did it really have to end up as a life and death situation? Were there no alternatives? The protection of your property, became more important than life. The fear of loss created that situation and created the belief, 'life sucks'. The second life where you died in the forest, could you have moved away from the forest to a much better area, because the forest was causing you breathing problems and you died because of it. You had become attached to the forest as it was your area. If you had moved a long way away to cleaner air you could have survived, but life sucks and caused your death.

Z. I didn't think so.

C. Ask your guide?

Z. Maybe if I'd moved a long long way away.

C. And the third life, you as a knight believed in honour, who went on the crusade and you wouldn't kill people. You refused to fight because it was wrong to kill, yet you lost the most important thing, your life.

Ask your guide is the fear of loss in each of these lives causing the problem, your belief that you will lose. Ask your guide can you change that?

Z. She says yes, it's a matter of belief.

C. So have you come into this life to prove that whatever you get, someone else can take. Have you come into this life to put yourself down and know that life sucks. We're going to change that because you can have the things you want. First you must forgive yourself for coming in with that belief. Can you do that? Can you forgive yourself for holding onto a belief that goes back many lifetimes?

Z.   With the help of my guide, yes.

C.   In this case will you ask your guide to stand on your left-hand side and whenever you say her name, she will be standing there and she will support you in all that you do.

I went on to discuss with her how she can change her beliefs with the help of her guide. How to achieve the things she wants and to feel safe knowing that anything she wants to keep, will not be taken from her.

FORGIVE YOURSELF AND OTHERS IS THE GREATEST HEALING YOU CAN GIVE

ADOPTION

This is an interesting case because she gives us information into the concept of adoption.

This woman came to me because she was overweight and in fixing this problem, under hypnosis, we went back to when she was first born and she told us she was to be adopted. So, the adoption was prearranged by her before she came to earth.

She actually came to the birth mother, who was the daughter of the person she wanted to be with (a person she called Granny). Unfortunately, the birth mother was not able to look after the child and her mother (Granny) was actually the person with whom she wanted to associate.

During the case study we found that Granny was associated with her in a previous life when the client was a man called Tom and had a close relationship with Granny.

Let's look at the case study.

        Z. is Client   C. is Counsellor

Z.   I just see a baby, I'm in a hospital and its cold, my name is Rebecca and I'm frightened.

C.   What are you frightened of?

Z. It's not the right place!

C. What do you mean, it is not the right place?

Z. The person who carried me is not the person I want to live with.

C. What do you mean, are you going to be adopted?

Z. Yes

C. Why are you going to be adopted?

Z. Because the person who had me can't look after me.

C. Let's go forward a little bit in time and see what happened?

Z. I was left in the hospital three months, it took such a long time, I'm very confused.

C. Why was that?

Z. Because the lady who was supposed to adopt me was pregnant and they didn't think it was good to adopt a baby when she was about to have one.

C. How did that make you feel?

Z. The waiting was awful.

C. Do we need to know any more about that time?

Z. Yes

C. Take us to the next important point we need to know about.

Z. We are back in the hospital. Granny wanted to take me but they wouldn't let her, they kept telling her I was too sick. I wasn't sick, they didn't want Granny to have me although I wanted to be with Granny.

C. You finally get adopted?

Z. Yes, the pregnant woman took me after the birth of her child.

C. So she ended up with two babies, how did that make you feel. Was there any competition, did you get less treatment?

Z. Yes, sometimes I felt disadvantaged and I felt I should have gone with Granny, but I didn't.

C. What decision did you make about life at that time?

Z. You have to be good.

C. Now we need to go to the next important point because we want to find out what causes your weight problem. Can you take this to the next important point?

Z. I am seven I was wearing shorts and T-shirt and I'm very anxious.

C. Why are you anxious? Can you tell me why you are anxious?

Z. I've done something to upset them and I couldn't go to Granny's.

C. So what did you do?

Z. I ate something I wasn't supposed to.

C. So you ate something that you weren't supposed to, so they stopped you from going to Granny's. How do you feel about that, and what decision did you make about life at that time?

Z. They are not going to control me anymore, but I have to be careful and be good otherwise they won't love me.

C. So you have to be good or they won't love you and do what they want, even though you don't like to be controlled. How does that make you feel?

Z. It's unfair.

C. So they should love you no matter what?

Z. Yes. I made the decision when I got older, I would eat what I like and they should love me, no matter what.

C. To sum it up, you came into this life to a mother who couldn't look after you. In fact, you chose her so you could get to Granny, which is the person you wanted to be with.

That couldn't happen so you were adopted by someone else who then let you visit your Granny which is what you really wanted, but when they punished you for not eating correctly, you made the decision that when you were older you would eat whatever you like and felt they should still love you and you could be with Granny who loved you.

I said she needed to forgive her natural birth mother for giving her away as this showed true love. Then she needed to forgive her adopted parents for any involvement with her, because they were only doing what they felt was right. Finally, she had to forgive herself for making a decision that people should still love her even if she was overweight. Now she can eat wisely and go back to normal weight and she would be loved. She no longer had to prove that even if she was overweight, people would love her.

ADOPTION IS PLANNED BEFORE YOU CAME SO ENJOY

WHAT HAPPENS WHEN WE DIE?

Let me start with a story, before I became a past life therapist there was a group in Sydney call TAD, they used to make technical aids for the disabled. On one occasion a request was sent to me by a friend who was a member of TAD, to make a device for a person who had muscular dystrophy. He was very well progressed through the elements of that disease, at the stage where he could not use his hands as they were too weak. He had a bed and a controller which would raise his head or lower his feet so circulation would be better or give a more comfortable position at night, without his family having to help.

I was asked to make a fitting where his controller could be installed and by using his feet left or right forward and backwards, he could control the bed.

I did this and during installation, I got into a discussion with him and he was telling me he was scared to die, he had been such a bastard, as he put it.

During his life he was a perfectionist and nobody could do anything as well or effective as he. As an engineer he would not let anyone help him with his job. Even at home if his wife did the washing up, he would immediately tell her how she did it wrong and redo it himself. The same way with his daughter, no matter what she did or was learning at school, he had to teach her the correct way. Everything had to be repaired before anything could be presented to school.

He was petrified that he was going to go to Hell because of what he did to people in life.

At this time, I was teaching people how to meet their guides. I asked him if he wanted to meet his guide and ask him what would happen when he died. I think he would have grabbed anything to ease his mind.

I was a little dubious, I had not met someone who was so much attempting to be in control of everything and I was scared that if I got his guide, he may be told he will be punished for his evil deeds. The interesting thing is, I had found on previous occasions having introduced people to their guide and taking the risk to ask their guide some of the questions that may have led to negative answers, I had never had such an occasion.

Guides were always positive, always saying that a person was on earth to learn, and told me that some of the illnesses people suffer, i.e. Muscular Dystrophy, have some of their skills removed to wake them up to the fact that nobody is perfect and they often need help, including him. If they do not learn from the warning, the illness seems to progress further and further to where the person has no choice but to ask others to help.

This was news to me so I took the risk and with a small exercise, introduced him to his guide. He relayed to me what his guide was saying.

The guide asked if he wanted to know anything. He said he wanted to know what would happen to him when he died. His guide told him he had had a strong belief in God. Unfortunately, he was not allowing other people to develop themselves fully. Every time he corrected someone and put them down, they would feel embarrassed until they learned their lesson, which was to handle the negative situations he was creating and move on with their life normally. At the same time his lesson was to help and assist others.

Of course, now in his situation, where other people had to do everything for him, this was his lesson to accept help from others.

He talked to his guide about the fact that he had been terrible to his daughter and his fear was, he would be punished. The guide reminded him this was a learning experience and when he went back home, he would learn through observation what he had done. He would learn those lessons because he would see how others could achieve and he should have been teaching them to do the job they were asked to do, allowing them to make mistakes, because no one on this earth is perfect and they wouldn't be here if they were.

I reassured him again that he would not go to hell because as a good man who had a firm belief in God, and God is love, so he would be fine.

I received a phone call about a week later to say he had passed away in his sleep and was now at peace. In the last week his life and attitude had changed dramatically, he seemed calmer and less stressed and treated people in a new way and thanked everyone for the help and love they gave.

Another incident was a woman who went back to a past life under hypnosis to where she was living in a log cabin in the country. She was on her own, it was cold, and she couldn't go out and get any wood for the fire, because the snow outside was too deep. She was lonely and depressed.

Not being sure what to do and wondering why she had such a dramatic scene, I asked my guide what was happening. He said, take her to the time after she died. Strangely enough it was that night she died and she was standing in a beautiful clean frock, next to her guide. I directed her to ask her guide why she was in that situation. To my surprise again instead of getting something negative indicating that she had been there because of things she had done, her guide said she had asked for a lesson in loneliness and all through her life she had been a lonely isolated woman.

She had no friends never got married and lived on her own in the country and struggled much of that time. She had grown her own food and lived with a herd of 5 goats, which she used for food. She asked, was I wrong to kill the goats? Is this why I was punished? Her guide told her the goats role in life is to help you, to give you friendship and also to provide meat for you to eat. Their soul goes back to a new life. They volunteer to come down again and to help mankind. You did nothing wrong and the important thing is, now you can look back on life and see what loneliness does to people. This is the experience you asked for. Then her guide said let's go to the next level where you can learn and understand why.

This is not an area where I would normally become involved, although on some occasions, the same as I did with this woman at the end of a session, I would ask them to go to the day they died and then move forward to after they have passed away. I would ask what is going on and they would tell me they are with their guide. On occasions they would even say they were with a close friend who had passed over. Occasionally they said there was someone that had been close to them and this is strange because that person in some cases was still alive, obviously we were talking to the persons higher self, the part that remains at home.

Then they would move through the light and have a great feeling of love. From there to the next level, where if the energy of the soul had been damaged because of some of the situations in their life, they would be counselled and the energy of the soul would be restored. They seem to be in a place where colour was vibrant, the housing where they lived was the perfect place they always wanted. All their tensions, worries, stresses and pain were removed. Then they would go to an area where their core group of souls reside. Then they could go through their life experiences and understand what had gone on and why and see how they had chosen that life to learn and grow as a soul.

A place where you will find out more about yourself than you could ever imagine. The interesting point is, as with all other parts of the universe, you have total free will. You make all the decisions while your Guide and the Elders are there to bring your attention to specific areas and also support you in every decision you make.

You are now in an area of total love and all decisions you make will be based on the love within your heart and soul.

You will now go through your life, word for word, action for action, through every situation you experienced and you, with the aid of your guide, analyse every event. This time not only will you feel the emotion you had at that time; you will experience the emotion of every person you were involved with at that time.

Simply put, if you got caught up in an event, positive or negative, you will not only understand your feelings, you will perfectly understand the feelings of the other people with whom you were involved. You will understand the effect you had on their life and the consequences of your actions, positive and negative will become very clear. This means you will then judge yourself and realise the pleasure or pain you have caused to others, and believe me, there is no tougher judge than yourself when you look at all the aspects with total love.

At this point you will start to have a list of all the things you need to rectify. Remember your guide's tasks are to bring your attention to the areas you need to look at and still they make no judgement.

 Peter, that would take a long time.

Peter laughed and said, That's okay, because you have all eternity.

There are some aides you can use, because in there are many levels of learning.

First one I will explain is the Akashic Records. When you go to the Akashic Records there is a specific book with your name on the cover and if you look around there are trillions of books. Your book is placed on a pedestal and when opened each page contains a three-dimensional image of an event in your life.

What you can do is touch any person in the image and you get the emotions and thoughts of that person. You can check around to see the emotions and thoughts of each person involved in that event, this gives you a greater understanding of how you affected other people.

By turning the pages, you come across different events in your life. This is handy because when you are in your learning group you can discuss different ways to handle the situation, which will enable everyone in the event to have a better understanding of what happened and also how to get a positive result.

The next area is what is referred to as The Tapestry. This is a large beautifully coloured tapestry that runs horizontally and looking to the left as far as you can see, is a record of the interaction of people throughout human existence. Looking to the right is only for the highly advanced souls. Each person who lives on Earth has a thread in the tapestry. Some of the threads are as thick as a piece of string, others as thick as your wrist. As people congregate together their threads move together.

The next area is the Hall of Records. This is a massive glorious building with white pillars and a look of total grandeur. This building contains the history of the world as it truly is, not the versions we are taught on Earth. It contains the history of mankind since its beginning. All the events the motivation, beliefs, lies, the expectations, pain, joy and the disasters, it's all there.

You asked what happens when you die, you go to a glorious place. People say to me, well if I go there, I'm never coming back, but they do. Strangely enough many people say under hypnosis, I'm in this life now and I am learning, I know that I can enjoy life and its challenges and I know whatever comes I have my guide and God to help me.

> **MAYBE YOU WILL BE BACK OTHERWISE WHAT ARE YOU GOING TO DO FOR THE REST OF ETERNITY?**

Message from Peter

NOW IT'S UP TO YOU.

I pray, as you move through this earthly plane, that you will understand the power of the Soul.

Appendix

Main Symbols

Above scene	Looking down from mountain or higher area means they are observers or uninvolved in the present situation.
At ground level	Involved in what is going on around them.

Colours

Red	Physical
Orange	Emotional
Yellow	Thoughts
Green	Peace
Blue	Love
Purple	Self-awareness
Violet	Universal awareness
White	Knowledge
Black	Problems

Colour of clothes

Top	Current learning or lesson.
Lower	What they came in with or have experienced in the past.
Flying above scene	Indicates the person is an observer and does not want to be involved in what's going on.
Sitting	Not moving forward.

On rock	The colours in the rock indicates area of problem.
On wood	How old. Indicates long-term problem.
On plastic	Colour indicates area of problem and that it is not a real problem, fake, made up.
Moon	A reflection and acceptance of someone else's attitude to God.

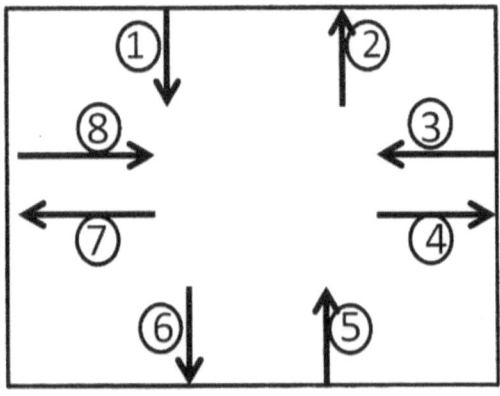

Moving	If something moves in direction of arrow:
Number 1	It is bringing it earlier in your life.
Number 2	It is moving it to later in your life.
Number 3	It is coming back from the past.
Number 4	It is moving into the past.
Number 5	It is coming from your early childhood.
Number 6	It is reminding you of your early life.
Number 7	It is delaying it to the future.
Number 8	It is bringing the future forward.

People

    Left side   Right brain symbols (intuitive).
                         People on the left side tells us the person is tending to listen to their point of view on intuition ideas.

    Right side   Left brain symbols (logic).
                         People on the right side tells us the person is tending to listen to their point of view on logical ideas.

    In front   Close to the person can either be helping or hindering progress to their goals.

    Behind   Indications of the past relationships. May be coming back into their life. Were they a good influence or a bad influence?

Position

    Left side   Right brain symbols (intuitive).
                         Problems on the left side tell us they need to use intuition to resolve the issue.

    Right side   Left brain symbols (logic).
                         Problems on the right side let us know they need to use logic to resolve the issue.

    In front   Close to the person are short-term goals.
                         In the distance long-term goals.
                         Any barriers indicate blockages to their goals.

Robert Todd

Behind		Indications of the past. Any barriers can indicate they are blocking out their childhood.
Standing		Moving or ready to move.
Sun		God and their relationship.

In front
- *Left* — Becoming spiritually aware.
- *Right* — Moving towards religious beliefs.
- *Centre* — Shows balance between spiritual and religion.

Behind
- *Left* — Losing spiritual awareness.
- *Right* — Leaving behind religious beliefs.

Things coming from
- *the left* — Coming from their future.
- *the right* — Returning from the past.

Things going to
- *the left* — Being delayed for the future.
- *the right* — Going into the past.

Walking (already on the move)
- *Moving to the left* — To a more spiritual awareness.
- *Moving to the right* — To a more logical lifestyle.

General Symbols

Animals
    Birds — Free thinking.
    Dolphins — Intelligence or wisdom.
    Horses — Strength, freedom.
    Sharks — Problems with a person.
    Other animals — Attitude and feelings towards that type of animal.

Beach — The larger the waves, the more they can handle or enjoy conflict.
The flatter the water, the less they like arguments.

Beach towel — Sitting or standing on a beach towel, is a barrier to the sand. Check colour of the towel to know what the barrier represents.

Boat — Goal, look at direction and check the colour.
If going forward, you should be on it, moving to the goal fast.

    Moving
    To the right — Is something moving out of your life.
    To the left — Is something being delayed from coming into their life your life.

Bridge — A way to cover over problem or to avoid contact with people. Made of wood or

Butterfly rock? Is it in front or behind to the left or the right? Look at the colour. Tends to flit from one thing to another.

Cages

    Behind — They felt hemmed in, in the past.

    In front — Indicates they think they have no choice and are bound by someone else's decision.

Car

    In car driving — Note the direction, if going forward, you should be in it, moving to the goal fast.

    Not in car — Moving *to the right* is something moving out of your life quickly.

    To the left — Is something being delayed from coming into their life or your life quickly.

Cliffs

    In front — Barriers. Feel they must lower their standards to achieve success. Or the person is an observer of life.

    To the left — Barrier to intuitive answers, fear of the future.

    To the right — Barrier to logical answers, wanting to forget the past.

Fences — Perceived barriers, may be able to see past. What are they made of, *wood* or *rock*?

Flowers	Opportunities, gifts. Have them pick them to receive the gift. The colour tells you the area of the gift.
Grass	Peace.
Ground	Look at the colour.
Sloping down	Will feel as if they are losing their self-esteem.
Sloping up	Feel they are progressing in the world.
Houses	Segmented knowledge. (The colour of roof and walls can give clues to area of concern.) (Look at first room in house to determine what area may need attention.)
Bathroom	Health.
Bedroom	Sexual relationships.
Family room	Family relationships
Kitchen	Food, diet.
Lounge room	Social relationships.
Mountains	In front, goals. Number of mountains indicates number of goals. *Snow-*
Capped	The long-term goal is a search for knowledge.
How far	How long they think before they will be achieved.
How high	How big or important.
Rocky	They see problems getting there.

Paths or walkways		Is it *smooth* or *rough*? This indicates their journey ahead. Look at the *colour*. Is it heading towards the front, the left, or the right of the scene?
People		Can be people they like or dislike. Look at the direction they are facing or going.
Pools or lake		In front can indicate they work with people, or they think their goals can only be achieved by working with others or others will help them achieve their goals. If some small pools around them, may mean they work with several different groups.
River		
	From left	New people coming into their life.
	From right	People coming back into their life.
	To left	New people being delayed from coming into their life.
	To right	Current people with whom they may be losing contact.
Rocks		Current problems. (Look at the colour of the rocks to determine area.)
Rock wall		Barrier blocking the way. (Look at the colour and size of the rocks.)

Sand

    Yellow — To do with thoughts. There are plenty of new thoughts coming to them.

    Golden — Indicating that God is around.

    White — Indication that there is knowledge for them to learn.

    Putting feet in the sand — Indicates they are trying to understand something.

    Picking up sand — Using their hands to dig in the sand shows they are trying to grasp new information.

Shells — A small surprise is coming soon. Pick them up and expect a gift.

Shops — What are you buying into? Look at the type of the shop.

Shrubs — Protection or barriers.

Snow

    On the ground — around them indicates there is plenty of knowledge available.

    On mountaintop — The long-term goal is knowledge

Timber — Old, long-standing problems.

Robert Todd

Trains
    In train looking out the window
        watching life go by without being involved.
    Watching the train
        Note direction, if going forward, you should be on it, moving to your goal fast.
    To the right   Is something moving out of your life quickly.
    To the left   Is something being delayed from coming into their life your life quickly.

Trees
    Single trees   Means knowledge, strength, protection.
    A few trees   On right can indicate the number of different areas of learning or careers.
    Trees multiple   Protection or barriers.

Water   A symbol of people.
    Colour   Of the water, green or blue.
    Rough   They don't mind arguments.
    Smooth   They like things calm.
    Cool or *warm*   The colder the water, the slower they make friends.

Waterfall   Knowledge from people.
    Stand under the waterfall to gain knowledge.

Solving Problems Using Scenes

A barrier
In front such as a rock wall, trees, or cliff.
To help overcome the current problem, look for a pathway around the obstacle, either left or right.
If you find a way round to the right, you need to apply a logical solution.
If you find a way round, or a path to the left, you need to use your intuition.
You can fly up high and see what is beyond this barrier. This will indicate what is for you waiting in the future.

Cliff in front
You are an observer. Fly or climb down to get involved.

Fences blocking your way
Look for a gate to the left or right and then open the gate.

To the right
A logical solution will come.

To the left
Use your intuition to come up with a solution.

Rocks
On the left or the right, or are you sitting on a rock? Then look at the colour of the rock to determine the area of the problem. Place your hand on the rock, and as you do the problem will

come to mind. As the problem is solved, the rock will reduce in size till it disappears.

Surrounded by trees
Not wanting to move from your present position. Look for a path in front to left or right-hand side. Follow to see what is beyond the trees.

No long-term goals, beach scene
Bring a boat from the left into your scene. Bring the boat ashore or fly out to the boat and stand on it to determine what your new goals could be.

No long-term goals, open land
Place a mountain in the distance. Then fly to top of mountain and put your hands on it and see what comes into your mind.

About the Author

Robert Todd ran his own training company in negotiations, interpersonal skills, relaxation, meditation and communications and was motivational speaker throughout Australia and New Zealand for 20 years he has also helped hundreds of people as a clinical hypnotherapist and councillor, introducing them to their guides while conducting past life regression.

**AS YOU TALK AND AS YOU THINK
THIS BECOMES YOUR LIFE'S REALITY**

KNOW THYSELF

These two words were written above the Temple of Apollo at Delphi, which was built in the year 320 B.C, and philosophers for centuries have continued to exhort us to know ourselves.

www.ingramcontent.com/pod-product-compliance
Lightning Source LLC
LaVergne TN
LVHW091933070526
838200LV00068B/757